Home Office Research Study 169

Addressing the literacy needs of offenders under probation supervision

By
Gwynn Davis, Department of Law; Brian Caddick, Kate
Lyon, Liz Doling and Julia Hasler, School for Policy Studies;
and Alec Webster, Malcolm Reed and Karen Ford from the
School of Education

University of Bristol

A Research and Statistics Directorate Report

Home Office
Research and
Statistics
Directorate

London: Home Office

Home Office Research Studies

The Home Office Research Studies are reports on research undertaken by or on behalf of the Home Office. They cover the range of subjects for which the Home Secretary has responsibility. Titles in the series are listed at the back of this report (copies are available from the address on the back cover). Other publications produced by the Research and Statistics Directorate include Research Findings, the Research Bulletin, Statistical Bulletins and Statistical Papers.

The Research and Statistics Directorate

The Directorate consists of three Units which deal with research and statistics on Crime and Criminal Justice, Offenders and Corrections, Immigration and General Matters; the Programme Development Unit; the Economics Unit; and the Operational Research Unit.

The Research and Statistics Directorate is an integral part of the Home Office, serving the Ministers and the department itself, its services, Parliament and the public through research, development and statistics. Information and knowledge from these sources informs policy development and the management of programmes; their dissemination improves wider public understanding of matters of Home Office concern.

First published 1997

Application for reproduction should be made to the Information and Publications Group, Room 1308, Home Office, Apollo House, 36 Wellesley Road, Croydon CR9 3RR.

Foreword

Literacy can be defined as being a set of tools for organising, planning and managing personal circumstances. As such there are few situations in society which do not require us to use these skills, and it is therefore likely that probation services will find that supporting the development of literacy among offenders under their supervision will complement their wider efforts to promote social responsibility and rehabilitation.

This report examines the priority given to literacy work by probation services and the extent to which there is a structured approach to assessing the scale of the problem on both an individual and area-wide level, the procedures for referral to specialist literacy support, and the organisation of such services. It covers the extent to which such procedures and programmes are monitored and evaluated, the funding arrangements for them, and provides recommendations for the future of literacy work in the probation service.

The findings indicate that the provision of literacy assessment and support is unsystematic and varies significantly between services, and even within them, though a few have begun to develop a more coherent approach to the issue. Few services employ their own literacy specialists, but instead use partnership arrangements.

The report concludes that a more systematic approach to literacy is required, taking into account current provision and good practice and clarifying the role of probation services in dealing with literacy problems. Suggestions are made for changes to probation officer training to improve the coverage of literacy issues.

CHRIS LEWIS
Head of Offenders and Corrections Unit
Research and Statistics Directorate
June 1997

Acknowledgements

This research consists of two elements – a survey and a more detailed assessment through site visits. The survey was the responsibility of a team from the School for Policy Studies led by Brian Caddick and Kate Lyon; the in-depth study was conducted by a School of Education team led by Alec Webster and Malcolm Reed. Gwynn Davis was responsible for co-ordinating the two arms of the project and for editing the final report. He was assisted in the latter task by Pat Hammond, Research Secretary in the Department of Law.

The research team would like to thank the many probation staff who contributed to the survey returns, and also those staff who gave generously of their time and their ideas in the course of our site visits. We are also indebted to Julie Vennard, Carol Hedderman and Ed Mortimer of the Home Office Research and Statistics Directorate for their support throughout the project.

Gwynn Davis
Brian Caddick
Kate Lyon
Liz Doling
Julia Hasler
Alec Webster
Malcolm Reed
Karen Ford

Contents

Summary

The research was conducted over an eight month period from December 1995 to July 1996. Fifty-three of the 55 probation services in England and Wales provided material for the survey investigation, while 11 of these were subject to the more detailed assessment through site visits. The object of the research was to assist services to focus attention on the literacy needs of the offenders whom they supervise and to establish practices, procedures or partnerships which will allow for an effective response within the service's statutory role.

Methodology

The first stage of the study involved the use of two different survey techniques: a postal questionnaire and a semi-structured telephone interview. Fifty-three services responded to our queries (95%). We conducted 85 interviews in all, of which six were with individuals external to the probation service.

The second part of our investigation involved more detailed examination of the literacy work of the probation service in 11 selected regions. We were granted access to a range of personnel including: senior probation officers; Employment, Training and Education officers; probation officers; volunteers; adult education tutors; and offenders. We attempted to discover how literacy services have developed over time, the object being to identify strategies which services might adopt to improve aspects of their literacy provision in the future. This was in recognition of the fact that in some areas literacy work is relatively well advanced whereas other services are only just beginning to address the issue.

Defining literacy

We define literacy as a set of tools for organising, planning and managing personal circumstances. In present-day society there are few situations which do not have a literacy component. Furthermore, our experience as researchers and teachers leads us to the view that literacy is best acquired in relation to specific social practices. This contrasts with a view of literacy as a set of skills, such as spelling or handwriting, which can be practised independent of context. Literacy is central to the development of logical problem-solving and is also critical in the achievement of social integration. For these reasons probation officers will find that practices which support literacy development will complement their wider efforts to promote social responsibility and reintegration.

Priority given to literacy work

The survey returns revealed a considerable degree of variation between services. Most respondents (58%) were clear that the level and type of response made by their service stemmed from the perceived relationship between poor literacy and difficulty in finding employment. Within the probation service generally literacy achieves the greater part of its meaning from its association with employability. The broad picture which emerges from the survey returns is one of *ad hoc* or unsystematic provision. If and when an offender's poor level of literacy becomes apparent, the action taken depends more on the staff member's interest in the subject and knowledge of local sources of assistance than it does on service-wide policies and dedicated systems. In short, literacy has a low profile in most areas of the service. Few probation officers could recall having addressed literacy issues within their initial training or subsequent professional development. Likewise, few had considered the importance of literacy in their rehabilitative work with offenders. Instead probation officers across the services visited concentrated on what they perceived to be the most critical issues for offenders in their care, these being repeat offending, addiction, and a variety of other personal problems including lack of accommodation, debt and domestic difficulties. Employment-related issues were considered next. Many of our respondents accepted that there is a connection between educational failure and the commission of offences, but few made the link between the particular learning demands of rehabilitation and the need for literacy competence.

The scope of the problem

Almost none of those who replied to our postal questionnaire indicated that their service had attempted to assess the overall scope of literacy problems amongst their clientele. Twenty-six services acknowledged that there was no mechanism by which a meaningful calculation of literacy needs could be made. It is likely therefore that the level of need is underestimated or poorly judged and that this contributes to the marginal status of literacy work. Provision made by services, such as the employment of tutors, tends to be on the basis of demand from individual probation officers, not on reliable estimates of literacy need amongst offenders under supervision in that area.

Identifying individual offenders with literacy needs

In the majority of cases identifying need is an inexact process. No service makes use of a reliable or proven method of identifying offenders who need literacy help. Except where it arises out of ETE assessment, identification appears mainly to be by informal observation. In most services literacy is associated with the employment, training and education initiative of Circular 40/1994. This raises the possibility that offenders with literacy problems may remain unidentified because they are in employment, or because ill health, disability or domestic responsibilities lead officers to conclude that employment is not a salient issue.

It follows that in most services offenders' literacy needs are identified, if at all, in an unstructured, informal way, or in the process of an assessment geared to employability. This hit or miss approach to the identification of educational needs reflects the background and training of probation officers who in most instances will have entered the profession with very limited knowledge of how to identify such needs. We noted also that probation officers generally did not have access to information from schools concerning the educational experiences or achievements of young offenders. Likewise it seemed that the educational profiles of offenders with prison records were generally not accessible or not consulted. Many probation officers expressed the view that literacy and its assessment were specialist subjects beyond their competence. We would agree that detailed, formal assessment is the preserve of the specialist. Nonetheless, probation officers could have an important role in the initial screening and referral of offenders for such assessment.

Referral and takeup

In none of the services visited apart possibly from Surrey were we able to identify a comprehensive and consistently applied framework for screening, assessment and action in relation to literacy. In most services referral for ETE assessment is at the discretion of the individual probation officer and is by no means automatic. The lack of any standard documentation reflects this somewhat haphazard approach to referral. The pre-sentence report appears to be the main form of documentation employed in the referral process, even at the stage of assessment and identification of problems by ETE officers. Even where there is a service-wide pro forma which requires boxes to be ticked signifying that education needs have been considered, it is left to the individual officer to decide what evidence to draw on when assessing these, and to make his or her own judgement as to whether these needs are critical. It is unsurprising therefore that there are probation officers in most services who literally never refer offenders for literacy help. A second reason for non-referral is a lack of knowledge concerning how to screen literacy competence (above), and a third difficulty is that many officers are unsure how to 'sell' literacy to offenders, some of whom may be reluctant to disclose literacy problems and be skilful at concealment.

The organisation of literacy help

While a few services have begun to develop a coherent approach to the provision of literacy help, the majority make do with looser arrangements in which different kinds of provision exist in different parts of the organisation, or some parts may have some provision and other parts nothing at all. Some of those who attempted to speak for their service on this topic had an unclear or partial picture of what was happening on the ground. Forty-four services indicated that literacy tuition, to whatever extent it might be offered, is provided by tutors from outside the probation service. Although this was the dominant pattern, our probation service informants held that provision not on probation service premises posed difficulties for the majority of offenders.

Thirty-nine services appeared to regard their existing or emerging arrangements as partnerships (although often in the context of employment or other forms of training). It was observed that the difficulty in securing external funding, and of ensuring its continuance, made the organisation of literacy help through partnership a tenuous business.

All services employ specialist ETE officers or their equivalent. By 'equivalent' we mean someone who assesses offenders' employment, training and education needs but who may not necessarily hold the ETE title and may not be directly employed by the service. Most ETE officers have a background in employment, not education. Of the services visited, only two had employees who were employed in the actual delivery of literacy help. More commonly services employed sessional assistants on an hourly basis to undertake a variety of tasks, including literacy work. It was observed that educational staff are not paid on a par with probation officers and are not regarded within the service as having equal status.

Literacy tuition on probation service premises mainly takes the form of optional 'drop-in' encounters with adult education tutors who work in one to one or small group settings on skill-based programmes which are unconnected to the other rehabilitative work of the service. We found only one centre where literacy tutors, ETE officers and probation officers work together on an integrated curriculum.

Monitoring and evaluation

Fifty services returning completed questionnaires stated that no attempt was made to monitor or evaluate the effectiveness of procedures for identifying offenders with literacy deficiencies. The implication is that the detection of literacy needs is not, of itself, a pressing issue. Had we asked about procedures for determining an offender's employment status it is likely that the responses would have been much more positive. Some senior managers, commenting on literacy work provided within what they regarded as a partnership arrangement, thought that the responsibility for monitoring and evaluating provision lay with the provider. There was no indication that the effectiveness of literacy intervention is reliably measured by any service. Nor are efforts made to assess the contribution of literacy provision to the other work of probation officers.

Funding

Our informants were unable to name specific sums earmarked for the identification and amelioration of literacy needs. We were commonly advised that the precise amount was unknown because it was encompassed within a partnership arrangement which included other elements. We gathered that spending on literacy was not a substantial element in partnerships or in ETE allocation. It also accounted for only a tiny part of the workload of most probation staff. It follows that the literacy needs of offenders do not yet command an identified presence in current budgetary debates within probation services. It is also noteworthy that many services are nervous about the long term consequences of partnership arrangements since the organisations in question are often supported by short term funding from outside the probation service. Even when funding is secured it is almost always precarious.

The future

The research demonstates that probation services do not have a clear, consistent or openly discussed view of literacy. This in turn leads to wide variation in the extent to which literacy needs are screened, identified, and planned for. There was no indication that the literacy needs of offenders are likely to be accorded higher priority by the probation service unless there is a clear lead from above. Indeed, most services saw a *reduced* direct role for probation in literacy provision, with a corresponding increase in the use of partnership agencies. Partnerships were disliked by some probation service managers because they were seen as symptomatic of the contraction of the role of the probation service, while the work involved in setting up partnerships was seen to be time consuming and difficult to fund. Even so the dominant view was that partnerships were the only way to bring about an expansion in literacy provision. The probation service could not, in the view of our informants, do everything that was desirable in meeting offenders' needs and it would require extra resourcing if literacy was to become a focus of future work. On the other hand almost half of our informants said that they would wish to see more provision, more flexibly organised, and with an element of in-house tutoring which in their view would help to improve take-up.

Despite the present limited engagement with offenders' literacy problems, it is our view that the ability to address literacy needs should be an important component of the probation officer's professional armoury. A number of steps need to be taken in order to bring this about.

First, it is important for all services to develop an overview of what they currently provide in terms of literacy intervention; a policy which identifies specific objectives; and a plan of action which sets targets and timescales. We provide detailed guidance on all these matters.

Second, the Association of Chief Officers of Probation (ACOP) could provide guidance, through its Training Committee, on the place of literacy work within probation practice.

Third, it would be helpful for services to have clear statements from the Home Office on:

• how literacy may be defined more broadly in relation to offenders' personal organisation, social responsibility and reintegration

• the role of the service in screening for literacy needs, referring offenders for detailed ETE assessment, and securing and evaluating literacy provision

• literacy intervention as an integral part of rehabilitative programmes.

Fourth, whatever the eventual form of initial training for entry into the profession, literacy issues should be a component of all training routes. Training should make explicit the place of literacy in the rehabilitative work of probation officers and should highlight the association between offending and educational failure. Any new training scheme should have a core of theory which is complemented by relevant practical skills. For example, all probation officers should be able to undertake initial screening of literacy difficulties with accuracy and confidence. Training should include the planning and delivery of rehabilitation programmes in collaboration with literacy specialists.

Fifth, probation service managers should engage in a dialogue with local institutions of higher education with a view to developing a range of accreditable modules with a literacy focus aimed specifically at probation service staff.

1 Introduction

The study to be reported here was conducted in two parts: the first of these was an investigation, using survey methods, of the extent to which the literacy needs of offenders are recognised by the probation service and feature accordingly in its involvement with those it supervises; the second was an assessment, through more detailed examination of practices within a selected number of services, of the strengths and limitations of provision within those services and the key factors affecting potential further development of literacy work. The research was conducted over an eight month period from December 1995 to July 1996. Fifty-three of the 55 services in England and Wales provided material for the survey investigation, while eleven of these were subject to the more detailed assessment.

Although identified as a consideration in its latest National Standards statement on equal opportunities (Home Office, 1995a), the literacy of offenders is not otherwise formally specified as a matter for Probation Service attention. The statutory purpose which guides the supervision of an offender – that the probation officer should seek to secure rehabilitation, protect the public from harm, or prevent the commission of further offences (Home Office, 1991) – contains no explicit reference to literacy work. At the same time probation services typically provide, on their own or in partnership with others, a range of programmes whose immediate focus is understood to be pertinent, even central, to the statutory task. It is possible to argue that literacy work falls within this category.

One form of this argument can be constructed around the truism that literacy can significantly affect an individual's scope for finding employment or participating in further training or education, supported by evidence, first, that unemployment and poor levels of educational achievement are high amongst a large proportion of offenders (Stewart and Stewart, 1993; Walmsley et al., 1991) and, second, that the literacy capabilities of offenders are lower than those of the adult population in general (Barnes et al., 1984; ALBSU, 1994). Grounds for attention to be paid to literacy might thus be said to be implicit in the assertion, in Probation Circular 40/1994, that 'offenders can more successfully be rehabilitated into the community and kept from further reoffending if they are helped into employment, education and job related training'.[1]

A second justification for a probation service interest in the literacy needs of those it supervises comes from research indicating that prisoners participating in basic literacy courses are less likely to return to prison. Palmer and Hollin (1995) have reviewed research dealing with the impact of education and work programmes in prison upon recidivism and, in the course of their review, highlight the findings of a recent Canadian study by Porporino and Robinson (1992). This evaluated the impact of a programme for improving the literacy and numeracy skills of prisoners and found that rates of readmission to prison were significantly lower for prisoners completing the programme compared with those who were released before completion and also compared with those who attended but then withdrew. These results are consistent with other, smaller scale North American studies. However an additional and noteworthy feature of the Porporino and Robinson research was the finding that participation in a basic literacy programme was seen by offenders as beneficial in enabling them to achieve significant personal changes relating to better self-control, better family relationships, and a sense of self-mastery and self-esteem. These outcomes have much in common with what the probation service has traditionally, and by a variety of other means, sought to achieve.

Thirdly, and more generally, it can be argued that literacy is inextricably linked with the potential for, and the processes of, social participation. This is not just a matter of having the skills to understand and reply to bank statements, job advertisements, questions in driving licence examinations, goods purchase agreements, television licence forms, insurance policies, benefits forms and the myriad documents which are part of day-to-day existence. Literacy should also be seen as that capacity which enables active and reflective participation in the world of words, symbols, communication, enquiry, understanding, enterprise and exchange through which a sense of connectedness and community can arise. It is, in other words, a core element in the development of a feeling of inclusion and identity with others and, as such, of underlying (if unrecognised) importance in encouraging the offender in the direction of re-integration with, and responsibility towards, those others.

But the fact that these arguments can be made is not the same as saying that the probation service has developed policies and practices which take them into account. Literacy, after all, is widely perceived as the province of the education services, and the probation service might understandably regard

---

1   This is the focus of a Home Office funded initiative under which probation services have entered into partnership with local Training and Enterprise Councils, the object being to assist offenders into training or employment (Roberts et al., 1996)

its own responsibility as being fully met in designing and offering its rehabilitative or offence-focused programmes in such a way as to make them accessible to those with literacy disadvantages. This would be consistent with the National Standards statement on equal opportunities mentioned earlier, though it would be more of an accommodation to a problem than an attempt to grapple with it.

It is generally held (though not reliably documented) that many local probation services have in the past provided support and assistance to offenders who expressed an interest in overcoming their literacy limitations. As far as can be determined, this was commonly a matter of officers or accredited volunteers offering *ad hoc* assistance with reading or number practice to individual offenders. Until the change in their role brought about by the 1982 Criminal Justice Act and, in some cases, beyond then, probation day centres may also have provided this or a more extensive kind of help and may even have made use of the voluntary or paid services of literacy tutors. But as the use of volunteers has become less significant in probation services and as probation centres have come, through legislation, to focus their efforts on a narrower proportion of offenders under community supervision, it is uncertain whether and in what ways these earlier initiatives have been built upon or developed.

In the meantime, too, the probation service has experienced a number of other changes, three of which could be thought to have a bearing on the attention accorded to the literacy needs of offenders. The most significant of these is the greater emphasis – first signalled in the document *Punishment, Custody and the Community* (Home Office, 1988) and promoted since then through legislation, inspection reports and consultation documents – on the punishment element in community supervision. As the opening sentence of one recent consultation document puts it: 'Community sentences should provide forms of punishment which are effective and which reduce the risk of further crime' (Home Office, 1995b). It is abundantly clear that addressing the literacy needs of offenders is not, of itself, an activity which can be encompassed within the 'restriction of liberty' and 'tough personal challenge' codes by which the probation service has attempted to meet punishment in the community expectations. To the extent, then, that services are re-directing their energies with a view to satisfying these expectations, literacy work may be accorded lower priority than hitherto.

On the other hand, the impetus given to the development of *partnerships,* both in Home Office documents preceding the introduction of the 1991 Act (Home Office, 1990) and in the subsequent requirement to devote a proportion of probation service funding to partnership arrangements, has opened up opportunities for expanded literacy provision. Jointly with local community agencies, or through direct referral to existing or tailored programmes provided by them, services now have available the possibility of building upon earlier, pre-1991 Act work by making more organised and formal use of the expertise available outside the service.

The third potential influence on services' attention to literacy is provided by Probation Circular 40/1994 with its prompts towards a more focused probation service response to the employment, training and education needs of offenders. Whilst literacy is scarcely mentioned in the Circular it is nevertheless clear that the strategies proposed would, if comprehensively addressed, generate useful information about offenders. This may in turn have led to proposals for new initiatives or for the strengthening of existing approaches. The recency of the Circular is likely to mean that any such responses would – at the time of the present study – be at an early stage. Equally, services may have decided, on the basis of information collected in response to the Circular, that literacy work commands a *lower* priority than other matters.

What the preceding discussion suggests, however, is that the literacy needs of a substantial number of offenders are likely to be significant and that there is a case for some form of probation service engagement with these. But the extent to which services have been willing or able to engage, and the considerations which will have proved decisive in this, have not been documented. As a result, examples of good practice and the scope for further development remain unknown. There has been little attempt to measure the effectiveness of such work as has been undertaken, whether this be in terms of improving literacy skills or in reducing levels of recidivism and unemployment.

Among the questions which we hoped to answer in the course of our study were the following:

- Are the literacy problems of offenders perceived as a matter of significance by the probation service? How central are literacy problems perceived to be to the effectiveness of offending behaviour programmes and efforts towards reintegration?

- Do procedures exist to enable probation officers to identify literacy problems amongst those whom they supervise?

- Are attempts made to record and measure the extent and nature of literacy problems amongst those supervised? How adequate are these?

- What specific response is made by the service to the literacy problems of those it supervises? Does this involve: specialist staff;

partnership arrangements or joint initiatives with other agencies or voluntary organisations; an existing programme in, for example, a probation centre; individual officer initiative; accredited probation volunteers?

- Is provision agency-wide or is it focused on a particular group of offenders or a particular geographical location? What procedures exist for referral to a literacy programme? How well do these procedures work? What is the take-up? What is the drop-out rate?

- How, if at all, does the service monitor its literacy provision and assess whether it is effective?

We hope our findings will assist services to focus attention on the literacy needs of the offenders they supervise and to establish practices, procedures or partnerships which will allow for an effective response within the service's statutory role. We aim to produce recommendations which will address the development of practice for services currently at very different points in their engagement with offenders' literacy problems.

2 The survey

Methodology

The first stage of our study involved the use of two different survey techniques: a postal questionnaire and a semi-structured telephone interview. The postal questionnaire was sent to all services simultaneously; the telephone interviews were conducted after the questionnaires had been returned.

The purpose of the postal questionnaire was to obtain basic information and to identify at least one contact person who could later be interviewed by telephone. The number of questions asked was deliberately limited (in order to encourage responses) and included requests for information about: the procedures in use for identifying and providing help to offenders with literacy needs; the means by which the effectiveness of these procedures is evaluated; the means by which the number of offenders with literacy problems and the numbers helped are recorded; how an offender's literacy deficiencies are taken into account when planning participation in various probation programmes; and whether any investigation of a link between literacy problems and the risk of reoffending had been carried out by the service concerned.

The questionnaire prompted a response from 54 of the 55 services in England and Wales. Two of the 54 said that other work commitments prevented them from completing the questionnaire and participating any further; the one service which did not return the questionnaire later participated in the telephone interviews. In all, then, 53 services responded to our queries (95%). Those completing the questionnaire included: 26 senior managers (ACPO or higher); nine middle managers (SPO); one research officer; and 16 others who could be characterised as employees having a special responsibility which (presumably) led them to be identified as the most appropriate person to complete the questionnaire. In this latter group were Employment, Training and Education Officers (ETE Officers), Development Managers, and others with similar titles and responsibilities.

The purpose of the telephone interviews was to confirm, clarify or extend the information obtained from the questionnaires, and to explore some additional issues either for the first time or in greater detail. We wished, for example, to get a sense of how services understood the problem of literacy deficiency, the level of importance they attached to it, and why they had chosen their particular response/provision. We also wanted to know whether they thought their current provision was adequate and how they would like to see it developing. Finally, we wished to gather information about the funding directed towards literacy and its vulnerability to financial cutbacks.

As we had asked in the earlier questionnaire for the names of other relevant contacts (as well as the identity of the person providing the response), we were able with some services to interview others more directly involved in supplying or arranging provision – mostly internal employees but also a handful who were external to the service. These informants were asked additional questions such as their views about the importance of literacy to offenders, levels of take-up and completion of relevant programmes, and the nature of their own involvement. Informants in 53 services were interviewed, totalling 85 interviews in all, of which six were with individuals external to the probation service. Forty-three of the probation staff interviewed were senior managers (ACPO or higher), 11 were middle managers (SPOs), and the remaining 25 held posts connecting them in some way with the topic.

Literacy as an issue for the probation service

Our initial expectation was that we would be able to gauge the significance of literacy as an issue for the probation service by the nature of the responses to our postal questionnaire. We reasoned that inferences could be drawn from a general tendency either to ignore the literacy needs of offenders or to engage with literacy in a committed and focused manner. What the postal questionnaire revealed however was a considerable degree of variation between services and, in several services, inconsistent indications of commitment between procedures for the identification of literacy needs and arrangements for providing assistance in addressing these.

In the course of our follow-up telephone interviews nine senior managers told us that as there was little demonstrated demand for literacy help in their area their service's response was minimal or non-existent. Indeed, one manager observed that literacy levels in the general population had increased and, since this must be true for offenders as well, no response was warranted. Five other managers said that their service had made no strategic decision about responding to the literacy needs of offenders but at the same time said that they regretted this or indicated that the position was about to change. The majority of respondents (58%) were clear that the level and type of response made by their service stemmed from the perceived relationship between poor literacy and difficulty in finding employment. In a few instances connections were made between literacy assistance and a variety of gains in attitude or competence including improved self-esteem, greater ambition, the ability to participate in probation programmes, and a reduced likelihood of reoffending. But none of these was referred to more than twice. Not surprisingly, very much the same pattern of replies emerged when our interviewees were asked about the importance of literacy in relation to the work of the service, and also when they were asked how the problem of literacy was perceived. With the latter, though, the stress on the link with unemployment was slightly stronger, with two-thirds making an explicit connection.

What these responses suggest is that within the probation service literacy achieves the greater part of its meaning from its association with employability. It is important to note however that nearly a third of all those questioned coupled their responses with the observation that offenders' literacy deficiencies were a low priority for the service in their area. Only one senior manager referred to it as a high priority, bracketing it with his service's recent efforts in establishing a more thorough-going employment, training and education package. Notwithstanding this latter example, it seems clear that the literacy problems of offenders are accorded low priority across the probation service as a whole. Certainly the picture which emerges from responses to the questionnaire and interview questions is of *ad hoc* or unsystematic provision. That is to say, if and when an offender's poor level of literacy becomes apparent the action taken depends more on the staff member's interest in and knowledge of local sources of assistance, or on a particular team's initiatives within its own patch, than it does on service-wide policies and dedicated systems.

Yet – apart from the odd response – it would be wrong to conclude that our informants were suggesting that literacy deficiency is an insignificant problem which is unworthy of attention. A handful did say that in their experience offenders with literacy problems had often learned to cope with their difficulties, but this was never offered as a reason for a low-key response and indeed many of those interviewed displayed personal interest in the issue and a keen sense of its relevance. We were also informed, in the case of five services, that new approaches were being devised or were about to be put into operation. Those who did put forward explanations for the relatively low level of attention paid to literacy problems referred to: low incidence (in some cases acknowledged as a probable under-estimate); a shift in probation service focus from 'life skills' towards community punishment and programmes for the control or eradication of unacceptable behaviour; and the common experience of having to respond to more pressing offender problems such as drug or alcohol misuse, lack of accommodation and debt.

Asked about procedures, structures and mechanisms for addressing literacy needs, there was a frequent admission that there are few formal ones in place, or that those which exist are components of a larger effort aimed at improving employability. Only a very small number of services are able to point to specific programmes established – or about to be established – on an agency-wide basis. But in comments offered, often on reflection, during the telephone interviews there are anecdotes about the known usefulness to individual offenders, much speculation that the matter may be more important than is being acknowledged, regret that the service is not doing more, and disappointment that literacy work once done in the 70s and 80s has been discontinued through its having been overtaken by other priorities. Indeed, nearly two-thirds of our informants, asked whether they thought what was being offered by their service was sufficient, answered with an unequivocal 'no'. This might lead us to qualify our earlier comments in order to observe that literacy is an issue with somewhat *ambiguous* status within the probation service.

Identifying offenders with literacy needs and charting the scope of the problem

The postal questionnaire invited respondents to describe what procedures, if any, were used to identify offenders with literacy needs. We also asked for details of how the numbers identified were recorded so that the overall scope of the problem could be determined. In some instances the responses were either partial or unclear and, where necessary, further information was sought during the telephone interviews.

What our findings reveal is, in the majority of cases, a rather inexact process. Although ten services employ a 'problem' checklist at the pre-sentence report (PSR) stage which includes literacy or educational problems as an item, no service makes use of a reliable or proven method of identifying offenders with literacy needs at this particular point. Instead, identification relies heavily on individual officers and so depends upon their interest in and definition of literacy. Not surprisingly, then, early identification does not always occur, in which case the problem may only come to light at a later stage in an order. (During telephone interviews we were told that literacy problems may be 'picked up' at various points: in the course of PSR preparation; by a supervising officer during or after the development of a supervision plan; during assessment following referral to ETE staff for employment or training advice; while participating in groupwork programmes; or, less frequently, through the offender's voluntary admission of literacy needs.) Failure to recognise literacy problems was accounted for in a number of ways by those who commented further: four of our informants cited a resistance to address literacy needs for reasons of supposed stigmatisation or intrusion; seven drew attention to officers' lack of appropriate skills or training; 21 said that identification is hampered because offenders with literacy problems are adept at masking their difficulties; and four blamed the lack of any formal connection between literacy and the service's statutory responsibilities.

Except where it arises out of ETE assessment, identification appears mainly to be by informal observation. Clues were said to be provided when an offender had difficulty with questionnaires at the PSR or supervision plan stage, difficulty with reading or signing supervision plans and reviews, or difficulty with understanding the content of letters or written instructions. Reluctance to write letters or complete forms and poor use of programme materials were also said to be indicative. This somewhat rough-and-ready approach was not necessarily regarded as deficient. Confidence in officer identification was expressed by informants from four services and two others argued that informal assessments were more acceptable because they were less intimidating. But, contrasting with this, we were told by a senior officer responsible for a literacy project in one area that a half-day's literacy awareness training had recently been provided for all officers and that a quarter of these were being given further training in identification. A development manager in another area outlined a project undertaken jointly with a local voluntary agency to develop a more systematic screening process which was about to be put into practice. (It was anticipated that all new supervisees would be screened for literacy at the same time as they were assessed for other skill deficits.) One other service supplied a structured and comprehensive assessment document, but its use was at the discretion of supervising officers which meant that it was not consistently applied.

Eighteen services referred to ETE activities (or their equivalent) as the context in which literacy problems might be assessed. But it is not clear from the responses how many *initial* identifications – as distinct from more detailed assessments following initial identification by a probation officer – are made in this way. Nine of the services citing an ETE connection indicated that the assessment was structured and systematic. But our questionnaire data do not permit us to say how many of these assessments are carried out by in-house ETE officers and how many by partnership agencies providing ETE-related programmes; nor, because of the variety of approaches adopted by some agencies, was it always possible to clarify this through the telephone interviews. What is clear however is that in many services literacy is associated with the employment, training and education initiative of Circular 40/1994. This raises the possibility that some offenders with literacy problems may remain unidentified because they are in employment, or because ill health, disability or domestic responsibilities lead officers to conclude that employment is not a salient issue.

Almost none of those who replied to our postal questionnaire or who added to their comments in a subsequent telephone interview demonstrated that their service had attempted to assess reliably the overall scope of the problem. The exceptions included one service which had participated in a recent skills audit of offenders on its caseload. The audit revealed that 23 per cent had literacy/numeracy problems. Another service had found that some 35 per cent of offenders given an employment guidance assessment were in need of literacy/numeracy tuition, while a senior manager in a third service referred to a draft report of a (now defunct) project in which it was stated that 37 per cent of offenders seen had literacy problems affecting their employability. Informants from seven further services said that information obtained at the PSR or supervision planning stage was monitored and that this information could be (although had not been) used to provide an indication of the size of the problem. But, as has already been mentioned, identification at these stages is haphazard. Moreover it was reported by some that literacy problems (if identified) were registered only in so far as they were judged to be offence-related. We were also told by eight services that ETE referrals were monitored, but again this could not be relied upon to produce an accurate estimate of the overall problem. Several others thought that an estimate could be made if data held within different parts of their service were (laboriously) aggregated. One service had, some years before, monitored offenders attending its probation centre and had found that over 60 per cent had a reading level below 11 years. Significantly, however, informants from 26 services acknowledged that there was no mechanism in place by which a meaningful calculation of overall literacy needs could be made.

It appears, then, that in most services offenders' literacy needs are identified, if at all, in an unstructured, informal way or in the process of an assessment geared to employability. It is probable as a result that the overall scope of the problem is underestimated or poorly judged and that this contributes to its marginal status.

Referral and take-up of help with literacy

In our postal questionnaire we sought information about how offenders are referred for help with literacy. Most services identified one referral source but some named two. Probation officers were said to be the source for 29 services, ETE (or equivalent) specialists were identified by 13 services and five services indicated that referral might be made by either of these. Informants from three services said that they did not know, and another gave a response to the effect that no referrals were made. Referral which results in literacy help is not always initiated in those terms to begin with: as previously indicated, unemployment may be identified as the significant problem, leading to referral to an ETE specialist following which literacy needs come to light.

It is also the case that identification of literacy needs does not always result in referral. Mention has already been made of the low priority accorded to literacy deficiency and the fact that there are often more pressing problems such as homelessness or debt which officers and offenders opt to work on. Among these problems there are some – like drug misuse – which can preclude any structured or focused work until a level of stability has been achieved. By then, too, the time remaining in an order may be so limited as to make a literacy referral unlikely unless there is clear motivation. Other offenders identified as having a literacy problem may reject the help offered. As one of our informants put it: 'Most are not very upset. It's not as though they're dying to read *War and Peace*.' Three others said that offenders are not willing to do anything about literacy unless and until they recognise that improved literacy can be of practical use to them. In addition, of course, literacy difficulties may simply be accommodated rather than directly addressed. Thirty-three services indicated that at least some of their programmes were deliberately offered in a form which did not require literacy skills or, if they did, on-the-spot assistance from a probation officer or volunteer was available.

In our postal questionnaire we also asked how many offenders had received help with their literacy problems over the preceding twelve months. Thirty–four services indicated that they had no aggregated data and that access to such data would be too difficult to obtain or that, as the information related to specific programmes or projects, it was unrepresentative of their service as a whole. Six other services did not respond to the question, while 13 gave estimates ranging from less than two per cent to greater than 10 per cent. (Nine of these 13 estimated under 5%.)

Most figures relating to help received are compromised, however, by what was said about take-up in the course of our telephone interviews. Thirteen of the 21 'internal providers' who were asked about take-up considered it to be poor, while only three thought it was satisfactory. Several different explanations for poor take-up were given by those who commented further. Five informants said that it was difficult to persuade offenders to attend literacy courses simply because these were a voluntary activity. Three others suggested that offenders were inhibited by poor school experiences and so were reluctant to attend external literacy classes where they feared exposure and belittlement. Four informants put a slightly different slant on this: not all colleges were willing to work with or make an effort to understand offenders, and tutors could be unwelcoming. This might be because colleges had minimum class sizes to achieve and haphazard attendance by those referred by the probation service could jeopardise the continuation of a course.

The negative attitudes of some probation officers were also mentioned in this context. Two senior managers were dismayed by officers' lack of interest in literacy as an issue. Lack of interest on the part of probation officers was also mentioned by informants involved in ETE provision. Some explained this by reference to what they saw as probation officers' excessive workload. This limited officers' capacity to give attention to offenders' literacy needs.

Suggestions for improving take-up focused upon the supervising probation officer and the need for that person to present literacy positively and thereafter to encourage, motivate and support the offender throughout literacy work. A few informants spoke of the value of having the probation officer accompany the offender during the early stages of tuition, whether that tuition took place in the probation office or in some external setting. Informants in three rural services made the point that the cost of travelling to obtain help would put some offenders off and suggested that a peripatetic tutor would improve take-up. (Interestingly, we were told of a metropolitan project which offers a 'student allowance' scheme to cover fares and lunches.) Some form of accreditation for having completed a unit of work or for having attained a particular standard was also thought to be effective, as was offering literacy help as an element within some other training package (e.g., computer skills) so that the literacy aspect was played down and made less embarrassing. Those who relied on external provision were most emphatic about lowering the hurdle posed by the transition between the probation setting and the external provider. Many offenders, it was said, needed pre-course, elementary assistance in which confidence-building was every bit as important as literacy. This, we were told, was most successful when the help was provided on a 1:1 basis so that reluctance about revealing literacy limitations could be ameliorated by the slower pace and a good relationship. But some of our informants regarded this as unlikely to be achieved in a service in which advise, assist and befriend had lost its centrality as a working principle. In the words of one ACPO: 'It is doubtful whether literacy can ever return to being a core activity of the probation service now that the emphasis is so strongly on public protection rather than any kind of rehabilitative work.'

The organisation of literacy help for offenders

In our postal questionnaire we asked for information about the way literacy help for offenders is organised. In only one case were we told there was no provision at all, but the information supplied by several other services lacked detail or was hard to decipher and it was generally necessary to obtain additional material or clarification by way of the subsequent telephone interviews. From these it became apparent that while a few services have begun to develop a more coherent and organised approach to the provision of literacy help, many make do with looser arrangements in which different kinds of provision exist in different parts of the organisation, or some parts may have some provision and other parts nothing at all. It was also apparent that at least some of those who attempted to speak for their service had an unclear or partial picture of what was happening on the ground.

Nevertheless, from the information we received it is clear that tuition – apart from help with the filling in of forms or participation in probation programmes – is rarely provided by probation officers themselves (although this can occur in probation centre or hostel settings or elsewhere when an individual officer has a special interest and acts unilaterally). Direct tuition by ETE (or equivalent) staff may also occur but appears, similarly, to be the exception. Indeed 44 services indicated that literacy tuition, to whatever extent it might be offered or arranged, is provided by someone outside the probation service. Tutors associated with further education institutions or local education services were most frequently mentioned (by 30 services), followed by staff from local training agencies (20 services), and then volunteers enlisted directly or through voluntary organisations (18 services). This pattern is consistent with observations made to us on a number of occasions in the course of the telephone interviews to the effect that probation officers are not trained to provide literacy tuition so it is more sensible to make use of those who are.

From the data obtained in the course of the survey it is difficult to be precise about the nature of the help provided. As was mentioned in the previous section, some assistance is geared as much to developing self confidence as it is to improving literacy skills. Some assistance, too, seems to be designed to enable the student to benefit from some other form of training (e.g. basic computer skills). A few services mentioned tuition geared to helping offenders gain City & Guilds 'Word Power' and 'Number Power' awards. But perhaps because so much of what is offered is provided by tutors outside the probation service, little is known about course content.

It is also hard to be precise about the nature of the arrangements by which tutors are engaged to provide assistance. 'Partnership' was a term used frequently by our telephone informants but it is not completely clear – in part because we did not seek a definitive statement – whether these are partnerships based on a contractual purchase of services (as per the 1992 Home Office paper *Partnership in Dealing with Offenders in the Community: A Decision Document*), or a joint initiative which may or may not have a contractual basis (as described in Circular 40/1994), or some looser arrangement whereby tuition, if requested, will be provided in a flexible manner by volunteers from outside organisations or by education tutors recruited from local colleges and paid at the going sessional rate.[1] What is clear, however, is that 39 services appear to regard their existing or emerging arrangements as partnerships (though often in the context of partnerships centring around employment or other forms of training) and that the term is used when referring to arrangements which involve further education colleges, adult or youth education services, or local training agencies. It is also used with reference to resources which might be provided or brokered by NACRO, Apex, ALBSU, SOVA, a TEC, or some similar but more localised unit. It is *not* used when referring to freelance tutors or to help provided by the service's own volunteer contingent, but some services make use of these *as well as* one or more of the outlets mentioned above. It can be seen therefore that the picture as a whole is extremely complex.

In the course of our telephone interviews we were offered various comments about difficulties or problems that had been encountered, many reflecting offender reluctance to accept referral. As has been noted earlier, it was said that this may be because transportation is costly, because the class-room atmosphere is unwelcoming, or because previous school experiences act as a deterrent. Thus while some of our informants favoured the use of facilities provided by colleges and training agencies because they helped offenders to become more aware of community services and more integrated within their community, it was argued by others that offender-paced, one-to-one help on probation service premises was more likely to be effective. Four of our informants observed that the difficulty of securing external funding, and of ensuring its continuity, made the provision and organisation of literacy help through partnership a tenuous business. Nine others, responsible for rural or sparsely populated areas, pointed to the lack of external expertise on which they could draw. One service, on the other hand, encompassed six education departments and remarked on the difficulty in establishing partnerships which were consistent across the area in terms of the amount of literacy help to be provided.

Evaluation and monitoring

Services were asked to describe how they monitored and evaluated the effectiveness of their procedures for identifying offenders with literacy problems and how they evaluated the effectiveness of the literacy help provided. We raised the question of evaluation again during our telephone interviews and also asked how individual progress was assessed. Our findings suggest that very little is done in either of these respects.

---

1   The term 'partnership' is also employed by some services when referring to bids for outside funds when, as is often the case, these applications are made in collaboration with some other agency.

It has already been pointed out that most services rely on probation officers or, in a smaller number of cases, ETE staff to identify offenders with literacy needs and that the process of identification – at least by the former – tends to be unstructured and informal. It is not surprising, then, that 50 of the 52 services returning completed questionnaires stated that no attempt was made to monitor or evaluate the effectiveness of procedures for identifying offenders with literacy deficiencies. One telephone informant commented sardonically that an improvement in the effectiveness of identification might simply result in new demand which his service could not possibly meet. But the broader implication is that the effective detection of literacy needs is not, of itself, a pressing issue. Had we asked about the monitoring and evaluation of procedures for determining an offender's employment status (which, it must be remembered, is the context in which literacy achieves meaning for many services) it is likely that the responses would have been much more positive. But it can hardly be argued that determining employment status is a sufficient first step in the assessment of the literacy needs of all those subject to community sentences.

Forty-five services indicated on their questionnaire returns that the effectiveness of their literacy provision was not monitored or evaluated. In the course of our telephone interviews seven services told us that literacy help could (in principle) be monitored during the overall evaluation of ETE provision but that since literacy help forms such a small part of that provision it was unlikely to be looked at. Two senior managers argued that literacy help need only be evaluated when such assistance is specified as a condition of a probation order; since that was never the case, evaluation was unnecessary. Three other senior managers, commenting on help provided within what they regarded as a partnership arrangement, thought that the responsibility for monitoring and evaluating provision lay with the provider.

A handful of services indicated in their questionnaire returns that the effectiveness of literacy provision was monitored through information about individual progress or achievement. The telephone interviews revealed, as might be expected, that whilst individual progress is indeed monitored, this does not provide a reliable measure of progress on the literacy front. It is probable that many services could, albeit with difficulty, collect and analyse individual records for this purpose, but there is no evidence that they do so. Thus it is conceivable that progress with literacy may go unrecorded or else be registered indirectly (e.g. securing employment). Indicators said to be used in monitoring individual progress include: successful progress into;

- employment or education;

- course attendance and completion;

- increased confidence;

- improved behaviour;

- qualifications obtained;

- or standards of literacy achieved.

Each of these might have a role in assessing the effectiveness of literacy provision, but some are suspect (e.g. attendance figures) and others are difficult to quantify (e.g. increased confidence). There is, then, no indication that the effectiveness of literacy intervention is reliably measured by any service.

During the telephone interviews informants were asked whether any formal attempts had been made to assess the contribution of literacy provision to the main work of their service. No such efforts were recalled, but a third of those who were asked this question went on to add that they personally believed that literacy provision was helpful. Some specifically mentioned its role in relation to employability; others commented variously (but less frequently) on the value of literacy work in helping to build confidence, in improving social participation, in assisting participation in groupwork programmes, and in reducing the likelihood of reoffending. A question we had asked in our postal questionnaire prompted responses indicating that at least 11 services were aware of research indicating that literacy was a problem for a significant proportion of offenders. This pattern may reflect the fact that the probation service does not in general conduct evaluations based on outcome measures; rather, it tends to think in terms of identifying a need and providing a service to meet that *need.* The very fact that a provision has been made available constitutes 'success' in these terms; provided the need has been correctly identified, and a provision created which may plausibly be thought to address that need, evaluation in terms of measuring the *effectiveness* of the intervention tends not to be accorded high priority.

Funding literacy work

As the responses to our postal questionnaire suggested that there were significant differences in the kind and extent of provision made by services we thought that it would be useful to know how much money services had allocated to literacy work and whether such funding would be vulnerable in the event of resource cutbacks.

When asked about the amount of money earmarked for the identification and amelioration of literacy needs, just over half our informants gave responses which were of the sort: 'unknown', 'none specifically', 'none directly', 'unquantifiable'. In each case these responses were qualified by a comment to the effect that the precise amount was unknown because it was encompassed within a partnership arrangement which included more substantial elements, or within funding designated more broadly for ETE purposes, or – less frequently – because such work was only one of a number of tasks which might be undertaken by individual officers or by hostel or probation centre workers. Implicit in these replies was a belief that the proportion of funding which might, with effort, be shown to be linked specifically to literacy-related work would be small. Indeed, the remaining responses to our question about the amount of funding were of the sort: 'very small', 'very little', 'minimal' and, in two cases, 'none'. The clear sense, again, was that spending on literacy was not a substantial element in a larger partnership or ETE allocation, or accounted for only a limited and often unpredictable part of the workload of mainstream staff.

As indicated above, our findings do not permit a definitive statement to be made as to the breakdown of funding between the so-called mainstream 80/20 budget, the amount which is required to be allocated to partnership, and any of the other funding sources recommended in connection with ETE development by Probation Circular 40/1994. However, fully three–quarters of the senior managers interviewed pointed to the importance of the latter two for resourcing whatever did exist or whatever it was hoped to establish. Eleven made specific reference to the possibilities provided by the European Social Fund, local Training and Enterprise Councils, or Further Education Colleges. For the most part these were being explored in the context of ETE work, the object being to keep costs down or preserve mainstream funding for other activities. Two of our informants made reference to joining with neighbouring probation services to negotiate external literacy provision, again as a way of minimising costs. In the same vein an arrangement 'in kind' (the provision of a room on service premises rather than a cash transaction) was mentioned in one instance.

Asked about the vulnerability of literacy work to overall budget cutbacks, over two-thirds of our informants were of the view that such provision as existed would be retained. This may be because they took the question to refer to cutbacks in the mainstream budget only and saw literacy work as being funded in a different way. Even so, the most common explanation accompanying their replies was that the partnership or ETE activities within which literacy-related provision tended to be embedded enjoyed such strong policy endorsement at the national level that its position was likely to be secure. (However, we have referred earlier to the concerns expressed by four informants about the difficulties of ensuring continuity of provision when funding is from external sources.) A handful of informants also remarked that the amounts which might be saved through a reduction in literacy work would be so small as to render such an action unlikely. Those who took the view that literacy work might be vulnerable thought that a squeeze on resources could lead to a retrenchment around what was called, by one manager, the 'core business' of the service. Three others referred to the reduced help that their services had been able to offer following the closure – for budgetary reasons – of probation centres. Only one manager commented that the vulnerability of literacy work would presumably depend on the demonstrated effectiveness of that work.

The message to be drawn from these findings is that, as an issue, the literacy needs of offenders do not yet command an identified presence in current budgetary debates within probation services. In the main literacy is an 'add on' item and a fairly ill-defined one. It cannot, of course, be deduced from this that the literacy needs of offenders are being ignored completely or that the activities undertaken are of poor quality. But it seems fair to say that a focused and systematic engagement with literacy, and the development of effective practice on a wider scale, will require more precisely costed, earmarked and monitored expenditure than is apparent to date.

Summary and conclusion

In the course of our survey we found pockets of engagement with the literacy needs of offenders, but literacy problems are accorded low priority across the probation service as a whole. The picture which emerges is of *ad hoc* or unsystematic provision. Taken with underdeveloped or non-existent information concerning the number of offenders with literacy needs (and the number of such offenders helped), a widely encountered vagueness about the funding of literacy work, limited procedures for evaluating the effectiveness of existing mechanisms for identification, referral and provision, and only pockets of interest in investigating the connections between literacy deficiency and offending, we reach the inescapable conclusion that literacy has a low profile in most sections of the service. At the same time we encountered considerable evidence of regret that literacy work has been overtaken by other priorities, and strong support for the view that its place within probation practice needs to be asserted and developed. The implications of this are considered in the final section of our report.

3 The site visits

Methodology

The second part of our investigation involved more detailed examination of the literacy work of the probation service in selected regions. By drawing on the questionnaire responses conducted in the first phase of the research a selection of 13 services was made from the 50 (of 55) which had responded by the end of May 1996.

Services were selected according to the following criteria:

- geographical situation (north, south, west of England and Wales)

- whether the service covered a mainly urban or rural population

- whether the service indicated a high, medium or low level of literacy support for offenders (although it should be stressed that the survey did not attempt to locate services on a continuum of quality).

Services considered to be likely providers of extensive or significant literacy provision at this pre-visit stage (Greater Manchester, Wiltshire, Surrey, Somerset and Avon) were visited first over a period of two days (unless near to Bristol). One service thought to be providing an intermediate level of provision (Gloucestershire) was also visited in this period. Services which indicated emergent literacy provision (Inner London, Nottinghamshire, Leicestershire, Cleveland and Mid Glamorgan) were visited in the final round for one day. Initial indications of high, medium and emergent provision were not always sustained in the course of our visits, reflecting differences between information provided by services on initial inquiry and that gained from face-to-face interviews.

Chief Probation Officers in all 13 services were sent a letter in which the objectives of the research and an account of its design were clearly stated. CPOs referred us to specific districts and centres within their service, and a contact person was allocated for each visit. Eleven of the 13 services complied with our request. We subsequently interviewed a range of personnel in 11 probation services across England and Wales between the end of April and the beginning of July 1996. The overall response to the project was excellent. Visits were well-organised and allowed us access to a range of personnel: senior probation officers, Employment, Training and Education officers (or their equivalent), probation officers, volunteers, adult education tutors, and offenders. Five services (Inner London, Leicestershire, Mid Glamorgan, Nottinghamshire, Somerset) invited us to interview senior managers, but in general we concentrated on respondents who had not been contacted during Phase 1.

We chose a developmental approach to the issue of literacy provision and support: how services have enhanced their literacy work over time. The purpose of this was to generate a range of strategies which services might adopt to improve aspects of their literacy provision in the future. This was in recognition of the fact that in some areas literacy work is relatively well-advanced whilst other services are only just beginning to address the issue. We were interested in:

- recent history: how and why a particular service has developed its literacy provision

- potential: how a service might develop (or sustain) quality in its literacy provision

- key issues: factors concerning literacy provision which need to be addressed by the Home Office and all probation services.

We shall be returning to this developmental framework in the closing section of our report.

The research process

Interviews were recorded on audio tape as a back-up to freehand notes made under fixed headings on a pro–forma. Most interviews were carried out by two researchers: one conducting the interview, one noting responses on the appropriate pro-forma. The relevant pro-formas were then written up in word-processed documents. Sometimes tapes were replayed in order to clarify events, particularly when researchers made one day visits alone towards the end of the project, and sometimes mininmal notes were made at the time, the researcher relying entirely on the tape to produce an account of interviews. Critical issues were logged and added to as the research progressed. The complete log of processed data has been drawn on to identify key issues and provide illustrative examples. Although we had intended to observe groupwork, tutor-offender interactions, and to participate in teaching sessions, such opportunities were not always available within the tight schedule to which we were committed. We were also aware of the risk that we might be viewed as 'inspectors' and so damage the student/tutor relationship. For these reasons we relied mainly on face-to-face interviews.

Area summaries

In conducting our site visits we gathered a great deal of detailed information which cannot readily be presented within a research report. At the same time we believe that the reader will need to locate our general observations within the specific arrangements entered into by the various probation services which we visited. We have opted therefore to present, as an appendix to this report, an account of literacy work in seven probation areas. All the main organisational arrangements and forms of engagement with literacy problems are represented in that appendix in summary form.

Defining literacy

As is indicated in the introduction to this report, we view becoming literate as critical to the development of a person's social competence. We define literacy as a set of tools for organising, planning and managing personal circumstances. Literacy informs day-to-day transactions such as pursuing openings for employment or accommodation (searching newspapers for contact numbers, registering with an agency, understanding and completing tenancy agreements or contracts). Sophisticated levels of literacy competence are often drawn on for everyday purposes such as reading an electricity bill, finding an error and drafting a reply. In present day society there are few situations which do not have a literacy component. In order to carry out the work of a tyre fitter, for example, a person has to be able to key data into a computer in order to produce customer documentation.

Being literate is much more than just acquiring the technical skills of encoding and decoding print. The examples given here indicate that literacy is applied in particular ways in given contexts. Furthermore, our own experience as researchers and teachers leads us to the view that literacy is best acquired in relation to specific social practices. This contrasts with a view of literacy as a set of skills, such as spelling or handwriting, which can be practised in isolation or independent of context. Because of the way in which thinking through written language helps people to plan, to reflect, and to revise, literacy is central to the development of mature, logical problem-solving.

Furthermore, as is likewise pointed out in the introductory section of this report, literacy is critical in the development of a sense of membership of a community. It is a core element in promoting active and reflective participation in the world of words, symbols, representations and social transactions. In our view, then, literacy is fundamental in enabling individuals to achieve self-mastery and self-esteem and to feel included in the social activities, procedures and economic exchanges of other community members. For these reasons probation officers will find that practices which support literacy development will also complement their wider efforts to promote social responsibility and reintegration.

Literacy in National Guidelines

Circular 40/94 is recognised by the senior managers of probation services and of partnerships as the key guidance concerning employment training and education. There is only one reference to literacy in this document (40/94: Section II, paragraph 13) and it appears in relation to the *assessment* of offenders, as one example of offenders' potential needs. The wider context embracing this reference concerns offenders' *access to employment* and employment-related training. The ACOP Advice on ETE issues is also cited, and the single reference to literacy here appears in the context of preparatory *vocational qualifications* in relation to basic workforce skills.

Services are not provided with advice concerning provision of literacy support at a national level. This is in a sense unsurprising because it is essentially up to local services to address their rehabilitative goals through whatever strategies they deem to be appropriate. Nonetheless it is open to the Home Office to signal that in its view literacy merits greater priority. As one Assistant Chief Probation Officer stated:

> "The Home Office should specifically request areas to pay attention to the issue of literacy because it is so easy with all the other things we are expected to do to lose sight of it."

Most interviewees, particularly at senior level, corroborated this statement. We were not offered any examples of policy documentation specific to literacy provision. Many elements of literacy support were in operation before Circular 40/94. Due to the lack of prioritising at national level, local services struggle to justify the place of literacy support amidst the various other issues which are given priority in Circular 40/94 and in National Standards.

How probation services define literacy

Since literacy is not explicitly considered by probation services, most respondents found it hard to define what they meant by it, generally drawing on public definitions gathered from media accounts and personal experience. Few probation officers could recall having addressed literacy issues within their initial training or subsequent professional development; most remembered a general social work module on 'child development' in which education seems to have played little part. In the absence of agreed, clearly-stated, working concepts it is not surprising that 'literacy' becomes a metaphor for 'general education'. Furthermore, in order to situate 'general education' within existing practice, even this metaphorical shift is frequently addressed in terms of 'reasoning and rehabilitation'. Few probation officers had considered the importance of literacy in their rehabilitative work with offenders. Indeed, none of the probation officers interviewed claimed to be confident in their understanding of what literacy involved. In two areas (Swindon and Oldham), there was a better-formed understanding. This had come about through the efforts of a local adult education tutor, supported by senior management, who encouraged a few probation officers to acquire qualification as tutors of Basic Skills through City & Guilds 9282 and 9285. However, definitions of literacy employed within Basic Skills are generally functional (spelling, handwriting, form-filling), with the result that most of the approaches adopted by tutors do not draw on recent ideas about literacy as a set of social practices which enhance personal organisation, problem-solving, logical thinking, self-esteem and social responsibility.

Priority given to literacy work

In the last decade a great deal of public attention has been focused on standards of literacy within the state school system. Two important constructs have emerged: a prescribed curriculum and a standard framework for assessment based on 10 levels of attainment. The National Curriculum and its assessment framework provide a common reference point against which the work of all schools can be judged. Probation services have no such common framework within which to locate their educational intervention.

There is a lack of curriculum guidelines relevant to the rehabilitative work of probation officers, and a lack of standard benchmarks against which educational attainment can be measured.

We are not suggesting however that the lack of curriculum guidelines is the critical issue underlying probation officers' failure to engage with the literacy problems of offenders in their care. Indeed, curriculum guidelines would be a meaningless concept to most probation staff and their managers. A lack of literacy provision for offenders was sometimes attributed to the fact that rehabilitative goals were in general downplayed in comparison with punishment. But equally significant in the eyes of our probation officer respondents was the fact of their many other responsibilities: providing reports to the courts; managing community punishments; and seeking to divert the offender from committing further offences. If the probation service as a whole accepted the part which literacy work can play in promoting its rehabilitative and anti-recidivism goals – not just in relation to functional skills but also in achieving a sense of belonging – then a higher priority for literacy might follow. At the moment however it seems that the majority of probation staff – although not all – view literacy very narrowly, as just one factor affecting employability, and this in turn means it has a lower priority than their many other tasks and responsibilities.

We found that probation officers across the services visited concentrated on what they perceived to be the most critical issues for offenders in their care, these being repeat offending, accommodation problems, drug addiction and domestic problems. Employment-related issues were considered next, including questions of job readiness, leisure management and vocational competence. Educational needs were considered last in most cases. This is consistent with the findings of our survey. Pressing social problems appear in general to be easier for probation officers to describe and provide for. A lack of suitable accommodation is more easily identified, for example, than an offender's inability to write to Social Services about benefit entitlements. Offenders may also be less embarrassed to discuss or act upon aspects of their criminality than to address aspects of their literacy.

It is also noteworthy that in so far as probation officers feel able to devote their energies to the processes of rehabilitation, literacy needs do not figure prominently. Many of our respondents accepted that there is a link between general educational failure and the commission of offences, but few made the link between the particular learning demands of rehabilitation, which is increasingly based on strategies for raising social cognition (facing up to and understanding the nature of offending behaviour), and the need for literacy competence.

There are three senses in which we can describe the priority given to literacy by probation services:

- **A covert problem**: whether probation services have a clear and consistent view of literacy which is openly discussed. In general the data suggest that probation officers have a wide range of definitions of literacy (mostly personal). Few services have defined what they take literacy to mean. Hence there is little consistency in the conceptual basis upon which services operate.

- **An uninformed problem**: whether there are consistent strategies in place to define the extent of literacy needs amongst offenders. In the services visited we encountered few effective methods by which the extent of need might be determined. The scope of literacy problems amongst offenders therefore remains poorly defined.

- **An unaddressed problem**: whether there is a coherent and systematic basis upon which resources are organised and allocated to provide literacy teaching for offenders. The data indicate that services struggle to know how to allocate resources appropriately and how to evaluate effectiveness.

In order to prioritise literacy provision a probation service manager would have to regard literacy as having a more than purely functional meaning in relation to rehabilitation. In particular, he/she would need to regard literacy as having a significance beyond its contribution to employability. We found few instances of literacy being understood and given priority at this level, although in some centres attention was paid to literacy support, generally as part of wider educational provision.

Perceptions of levels of literacy amongst offenders

No service was able to provide a systematic overview of the literacy needs, or even the broad educational needs, of their clientele, using educational testing or profiling. Literacy need was mainly described in general or impressionistic terms, involving the use of labels such as 'illiterate' or 'functionally illiterate'. Most non-specialists referred to 'many' or 'plenty' of their clients being illiterate, without being able to give exact or even approximate numbers from their caseloads.

Tutors working within probation services observed that many offenders were unable to admit to their true level of literacy competence due to a lack of self-confidence, a troubled relationship with teachers at secondary school, or embarrassment. Tutors reported substantial gains in achievement with their students when a learning relationship had been developed. For the most part the offenders whom they tutored were not so much illiterate as difficult to motivate and engage.

In national surveys (for example, carried out by ALBSU), one-third of adults are typically described as 'marginally literate' - they have some skills but not the full range of competencies. It would seem that most offenders fall within this group. Although we asked probation officers and tutors to make estimates of literacy need, there is little precision in these data which are largely based on personal intuition. Provision made by services, such as the employment of tutors, tends to be on the basis of demand from selected POs, not on reliable estimates of literacy need amongst offenders under supervision in that area.

The offender perspective

We did not set out to gain an in-depth account of offenders' perspective on literacy. However, in the course of our visits we took the opportunity to gain some insight into how the offender/student perceived literacy issues. A total of 12 male offenders aged 18 to late 40s were interviewed, these interviews being conducted in nine of the 11 services visited. Each had recent experience of participation in literacy provision of some kind. Although individuals had different life experiences and a variety of reasons for accessing literacy provision, their life histories often followed a common 'script' or profile. Most came from families where there was little encouragement to develop literacy (presence of books, newspapers, story-reading, library membership). In general there was poor quality family support (homework support, rapport with school). Seven of those interviewed attributed this to having only one carer (usually a mother) who was said to be pre-occupied with maintaining an income for survival. For others parental support altered dramatically with changing social and economic circumstances such as the departure of a parent. Some offenders reported a parental belief that education was the 'school's job'. Beyond parents, there were few examples of significant adults who had encouraged them to learn.

On entry to primary school some interviewees reported feeling that they were starting learning at a level below that of the rest of the class. As they moved through the school system literacy and other difficulties became more noticeable, more difficult to conceal, and therefore more problematic. By the secondary phase most interviewees reported getting into trouble and absconding. Five of those interviewed had their difficulties recognised to some degree, and interventions resulted. Several had been placed in a special class, described as being for backward or badly behaved pupils. Two had attended boarding school and had found the experience more positive than their previous schooling. However, for those placed in special classes the experience simply served to reinforce the notion that school was unproductive as far as they were concerned. All left school before undertaking exams to avoid certain failure, although in reality they had ceased participating much earlier.

Few offenders could recall positive interactions with school teachers. The few positive memories concerned teachers who had recognised learning difficulties and had sought ways of working around these (e.g. the science teacher who assessed through discussion rather than written work). Despite the history of poor relationships with teachers the offenders interviewed did not blame teachers for their current literacy problems but often blamed themselves. Most felt that their difficulties were due to their own lack of motivation or bad behaviour. Several regretted not having achieved more at school.

Offenders' predominantly negative perceptions of schooling affected their attitude to continuing education to such an extent that they were often reluctant to undertake whatever was offered to them by the probation service. In believing that they were incapable of learning or achievement, most harboured a real fear of failure. Of those interviewed who had had prison experience, some reported the need to communicate with their families or to occupy their time as important motivations for improvement.

The organisation of literacy work

Figure 3.1 provides an overview of the range of personnel responsible for literacy provision, summarises the way this is organised in relation to external organisations such as FE colleges or partnership bodies, and indicates the typical qualifications possessed by those involved. It must be emphasised that within a given probation service there may be more than one type of provision, and that different categories of personnel may be involved in delivering this. Within single centres or districts a variety of initiatives have grown, often driven by a single person or a small group of like-minded people with a concern for education. This is illustrated by the Oldham provision which has grown from a partnership between the Oldham Day Centre staff and the Oldham Youth and Community Education Service (OYCES). In the absence of a clear national policy it is up to individuals to create practices which may then be defended in future policy statements.

Figure 3.1: The organisation of literacy support

Type of Personnel	General Description	Typical Tutor Qualification
Adult and Community Education Tutor	Tutor from community education organisation	City & Guilds 9282 Initial Certificate City & Guilds 9285 Advanced Certificate City & Guilds D32 Skills Assessors Local college ABE teaching course
FE Tutor	Tutor from a college of Further Education	As above
Tutor through Partnership Agency	Tutor who is employed either by - the partnership agency or by an external organisation (e.g. community organisation)	As above Can also include a degree or diploma in educationally related subjects, e.g. BA in languages
Probation Service ETE (or equivalent) or Educational Specialist	ETE with educational background and teaching experience, teaching in an education group, drop-in group, or one to one	As above Diploma or degree, e.g. RSA Diploma in Adult & Vocational Education B.Ed
Probation Officer	PO delivering group-work in which literacy support is provided	City & Guilds 9282 Alternatively, none
Probation Service sessional assistant	Person employed on an hourly basis, usually to provide literacy support for groupwork	Various, including: City & Guilds 9282 Teaching degree or diploma
Probation Service volunteer	PSV who may provide support in groupwork, an educational group, drop-in group, or in one to one tutoring role	Various, including: No formal qualification City & Guilds 9282 Teaching degree or diploma

In-house provision

Many of the probation services visited organise their own in-house provision (on probation service premises). This is done by employing tutors directly to work with individuals or groups of offenders on literacy programmes, by recruiting volunteers, or by recruiting tutors from local FE colleges. In Swindon, for example, literacy help is offered by an Education Co-ordinator, an assistant, six volunteers and a tutor brought in for two mornings per week from a local FE college.

The location of the provision is an important issue. While all types of provision identified in Figure 3.1 can be located either on probation service premises or at some other location (such as a College of Further Education) all those interviewed believed that having provision 'off-site' posed difficulties for offenders. Offenders with poor educational experiences are more reluctant to attend classes if these are offered away from probation service premises, especially if the provision is at an educational institution. When the BEAVER Project began in Nottingham in 1977 literacy support was provided at a college close to the main probation office. Attendance was extremely poor, following which the project was moved to probation service premises. This led to a significantly increased attendance. Where there is little or no in-house provision and the literacy support is provided at the premises of a partnership organisation (such as *Making Headway* in Middlesbrough), probation officers are encouraged by the organisation to accompany offenders to the first session so as to provide initial support. This appears to be an effective strategy, but is not always achievable due to the other demands on probation officers' time.

Those with in-house provision suggested that many of their students attended because they had been in the same building for some other activity (such as attending a day centre programme), during which they were introduced to the tutors or organisers of the educational provision. As a result they were able to find out about the literacy work before they committed themselves. In the case of 'drop in' sessions (for example, at the day centre at Bridgend in Mid Glamorgan) offenders' attendance was encouraged by their probation officer who would suggest that they might like to have a 'no obligation' chat with the Adult Education tutor who was already on the premises. At Woolwich (Inner London Probation Service) this method of encouraging offenders to accept educational support through immediate, on-site introduction to tutors was also seen to be successful. The opportunity to collaborate with educational specialists when screening offenders was seen as preferable to relying on individual officers to make referrals to an unknown provision requiring attendance on separate premises on a different occasion.

The role of the Employment, Training and Education Officer

When probation officers suspect or become aware that an offender has literacy difficulties the first step to securing appropriate intervention in many services is to refer to the ETE officer. All of the services visited employ specialist ETE officers or their equivalent. By 'equivalent' we mean someone who assesses offenders' employment, training and education needs but who may not necessarily hold the ETE title and may not be directly employed by the probation service. For example, the person undertaking the ETE role at Swindon is actually the director of a partnership organisation, Jobwise. In Nottinghamshire, four of the five people in ETE roles come from multi-funded partnership projects.

ETE officers employed within the probation service often work in collaboration with a senior manager in order to develop partnership schemes or raise funds. Circular 40/94 has contributed to an acceptance that criminality and a lack of employment possibilities are connected, and has tended also to lead to an emphasis upon employment and training *before* education. Most ETE officers have a background in employment, not education, and consequently have a tendency to address offenders' employment needs ahead of their educational needs. In only two of the services visited (Gloucester and ILPS) were ETE officers required to have, or found to have, teaching qualifications. Although many ETE officers across the services visited expressed a concern for educational issues, few were experienced in monitoring provision with a critical eye for quality. Of the services visited, only two had employees, either ETE officers (Gloucester) or an education specialist (Swindon), who were involved in actual delivery of literacy provision. These individuals had been recruited into the probation service on the strength of their previous educational experience and qualifications. Even in their case direct literacy work with offenders was only a small part of their role.

FE and Community Education Tutors

The FE and Community Education Tutors interviewed would normally have gained adult education Basic Skills qualifications, either through the college employing them or through other bodies such as City & Guilds. Several had begun work in the area as volunteers and had moved to paid employment, usually working for the same organisation. Many had gained the required qualifications 'on the job'.

Only one of the tutors interviewed was employed by a partnership agency (*Making Headway* at Cleveland) specifically to provide one-to-one literacy and numeracy tuition. Although he had begun as a volunteer (on a probation service project which then became an independent agency) he already had a BA in Languages and subsequently gained further qualifications in Adult Basic Education. Education tutors are often peripatetic workers who lack permanent contracts either with the probation service or with the local College of Further Education. The tutor interviewed at the probation day centre in Woolwich represented well the insecurity of the position and the long-term struggle over more than a decade to achieve specialist qualifications for his role.

Probation officers as tutors

At the Oldham Bridge Probation Centre probation officers deliver programmes in which literacy provision is integrated. These officers have all undertaken the City & Guilds 9282 Initial Certificate in Teaching Basic Communication Skills. The probation officer we interviewed had found this course valuable as it had given him understanding of educational principles which he felt were essential in meeting offenders' educational needs. A senior probation officer in the Leicestershire service noted the similarity between groupwork delivery of any kind and teaching, noting that most probation officers delivering groupwork had no teaching qualifications or indeed pedagogical background of any kind, although we should acknowledge that many had received training in facilitating groups. Of the small group of senior managers whom we interviewed, only one (the ACPO at Lewisham) had any training in literacy support, this having been gained as a probation officer in another service, under the direction of an Adult Education tutor. We should commend those few probation officers who have sought such further training and qualification. The content and emphasis of initial training and post-qualification professional development – particularly the inclusion of educational issues – are considered in the final section of this report.

Sessional assistants

Sessional assistants are employed by the probation service on an hourly basis to undertake a variety of work. Those employed to deliver literacy provision take different roles in different services, according to their previous experience and background. A sessional assistant interviewed at Somerset was an experienced educator and former headteacher, but delivered mostly one-to-one tuition. In contrast, the respondent at Oldham had begun as a volunteer and had undertaken the City & Guilds qualification once he had moved to paid work. Part of his current role is to deliver literacy assistance in the context of the probation centre programmes. Sessional assistants, like education tutors, are generally peripatetic. Historically this reflects conditions of service similar to those of classroom assistants in primary schools and some teachers of special needs in secondary education. The tendency for remedial education to be marginalised rather than integrated in the delivery of the school curriculum is a well-worn theme in educational debate. In the case of the probation service of course the marginalisation of literacy support may spring from somewhat different roots in that it reflects a lack of knowledge about the significance of literacy and its applicability to the probation service's core responsibilities.

Volunteers

The background and role of volunteers recruited for the purposes of literacy work also varies between services. As previously noted, many of those who are paid tutors began as volunteers. When asked about selection and recruitment of volunteers all services had some type of selection criteria, although details were not always available. The respondents interviewed who had at one time been volunteers had all received basic probation service volunteer training. All had chosen to work in the literacy area because of prior experience of or interest in education. Most had gained further specific qualifications once they began volunteer work. The roles undertaken by volunteers ranged from providing literacy assistance to offenders engaged in group work programmes who were identified as having learning difficulties (e.g. Leicester Day Centre's Challenging Offending Programme) to providing one-to-one tuition (Nottingham's Practical Assessment Team).

Relevance of recognised tutor qualifications

While the background and experience of those delivering literacy provision varies, it is evident that those in paid employment for this purpose are more likely to have Basic Adult Education qualifications. Some of those interviewed expressed the view that some of the recognised qualifications (e.g. City and Guilds 9285) provided useful tools for practice but were too reliant on a 'skills based' approach. It would appear that further literacy training which draws on a detailed understanding of the context of probation work is not yet available. We know of no universities or colleges which have sought to develop post qualification courses in literacy designed specifically for the probation service. We consider some of the implications for higher education institutions working with probation services in the concluding section of our report.

Status and conditions

Status and conditions for those delivering literacy provision varied between the services visited. One highly experienced sessional tutor reported working in what he perceived to be 'low status' conditions: no written guidelines, excluded from service meetings and case discussions, employed on an *ad hoc* basis as and when required, rarely consulted or asked for advice. In contrast others such as the college tutor teaching at the Gloucester Barbican Centre enjoy good classroom facilities with appropriate resource material and access to support equipment such as a photocopier and a telephone. In general it was observed that educational staff are not paid on a par with probation officers and are not regarded within the service as having equal status.

Funding

Funding for literacy varies both in terms of the source of the money and the amount spent. Gaining a clear view of how much is spent is further complicated by the fact that most literacy work is undertaken under the ETE banner which includes literacy amongst a range of other matters, notably employment. In the course of our site visits we noted that some services have formal contractual arrangements for the provision of literacy support. Some independent agencies have been set up specifically to continue existing relationships which were previously funded by other means. At Oldham the independent organisation is represented by a consultant who was formerly part funded as a project worker by ALBSU. Her role is to co-ordinate and teach on the Open Links Project at the Oldham Day Centre, where she is based. At Swindon the independent organisation *Jobwise* was set up by a former probation service employee as part of a joint project between the probation and employment services. This consultant is based at the Swindon probation centre and her role, which includes the assessment and referral of offenders according to their educational needs, is equivalent to that of an ETE officer.

Educational support typically takes the form of small group work. Provision may be in-house, as at the Barbican Centre in Gloucester, with some resources and facilities supplied by the probation service but tutors' salaries met by the college, or it may be extra-mural. A comprehensive range of resources and facilities (as available in Gloucester, where educational provision has been developed by an ETE officer over the last ten years) was sometimes evident, but in other cases there was a bare minimum (for example, space in a room at the day centre in Mid-Glamorgan). Several of the tutors interviewed provided their own equipment and carried it around with them because of the lack of suitable storage space. College-funded 'in-house' tutoring used to be more widespread. Changes in further education funding have meant small classes are no longer cost effective. This has resulted in the loss of such provision and a reliance upon other sources of assistance, mainly volunteers.

Internally funded 'in-house' provision

Several services offer literacy work 'in-house'. This can involve the deployment of ETE (or equivalent) staff in combination with volunteers and/or sessional assistants. At Cheltenham drop-in sessions are being piloted with teaching by the ETE officer and a volunteer who is an Adult Basic Education tutor from a community organisation. At Swindon the Education Co-ordinator, her assistant, a college tutor, and a team of probation service volunteers provide tutoring at the probation centre. In Leicestershire volunteers are deployed to assist in groupwork where this requires a higher level of literacy than is possessed by the offender. In addition to paying these staff (or refunding expenses for volunteers), the cost of teaching space, teaching resources, electricity and telephones also comes from the probation service budget.

Hidden funding

Some of the probation officers interviewed (e.g. Nottingham and Cleveland) suggested that some probation officers have contacts with volunteers through whom they arrange literacy support for offenders. There are also some officers with a special interest in literacy and other learning issues who undertake work with clients in addition to their normal duties (for example, a group of probation officers at Leicester assisted in the delivery of a programme for sex offenders with learning disabilities). The funding of these informal arrangements, either through expenses paid to volunteers or time taken by probation officers, does not appear to be considered part of the funding issue and could therefore be described as 'hidden' funding.

Funding awarded by bodies outside the probation service

Most of the probation services visited apply to and receive monies to fund literacy and ETE projects from a variety of sources. These include: the Single Regeneration Budget (European Funding); slippage money from a variety of organisations (e.g. local authorities, the Home Office); grants from local authorities under various heads (such as *City Challenge*); and various charities. The amounts of money requested range from substantial support for new initiatives (such as the Surrey Adult Education Project) to grants gained by individual offenders applying to charities (with the help of a probation officer or ETE officer, as in Gloucester) in order to meet costs incurred on college courses (for example, the purchase of books and stationery). While many of the services visited have a manager whose job includes seeking funding through these kinds of initiative, it generally falls to individual ETE officers to pursue funds to support new initiatives, often for relatively small amounts (such as the few hundred pounds required to continue the newly established 'drop-in' sessions at Cheltenham).

Concerns about the funding of literacy work

All the services visited expressed concern over the lack of targeted money for literacy work, and the lack of guidance as to how partnership money should be spent. Those in the process of developing literacy provision, such as in Leicestershire, were uncertain how best to spend the resources available to meet literacy needs within National Standards. Many services appeared nervous about the long term consequences of partnership arrangements since partnership organisations are often supported by short term funding from outside the probation service. The criteria for receiving funds are different for each organisation applied to, and may change. Even when funding is secured it is almost always precarious.

Identifying individual needs

The issues raised in this section are key to the development of literacy work in the probation service. In our view probation officers should be able to screen offenders in order to begin to identify those individuals who have limited competence in literacy. Good practice indicates that screening is an ongoing process which should have a number of components and draw on a range of evidence. For example, some offenders will have prison records and educational assessments may have already been carried out. In addition, it should be within the probation officer's competence to carry out simple screening tests, to elicit relevant information during interviews, and to observe critical behaviour in relation to the printed word. Probation officers could use a range of 'proxy' measures: asking an offender to point to the sections on a driving licence which denote which vehicles the holder is entitled to drive; checking comprehension of headlines or news reports in a tabloid newspaper; and observing offenders writing letters, filling in forms, or making applications. We would not expect that the majority of probation officers would be involved at the next stage; making detailed assessments of individual literacy needs, leading to an action plan. This is the province of the ETE officer, or of the literacy tutor with more specialised knowledge and experience.

We being by establishing a common language. We use the term *screening* to refer to the systematic collection of data on a population; for example, using simple tests or 'proxy' measures of literacy competence as a basis for deciding which individuals require further, more detailed investigation. Good practice in other areas where screening is carried out (such as screening pre-school children for hearing loss) suggests that an effective screening programme does not rely solely on one instrument used at one point in time. *Assessment* refers to a more precise investigation, often deploying special test measures, of selected aspects of individual competence (such as a measure of reading comprehension) in order to give a more precise judgement on the nature of any difficulties and how these might be resolved. By *identification* we mean the process of verifying individual needs – for example, the categorisation of literacy competencies according to agreed criteria.

Role of probation officers in the screening process

Probation officers are key agents in determining whether offenders have access to appropriate literacy intervention and how this is integrated with the other work of the service. Detection of literacy difficulties depends on probation officers being informed about literacy competencies and alert to the possibility that some offenders will have unmet literacy needs. At an informal level awareness of literacy needs will depend on the officer's understanding of what literacy means, and of the circumstances in which literacy competencies can be observed. The current 'hit or miss' approach to the identification of educational needs partly reflects the background and training of probation officers, most of whom may have entered the profession with very limited knowledge of how to identify such needs.

Referral in practice

In none of the services visited were we able to observe a consistently applied framework for screening, assessment, identification and action in relation to literacy. Referral for ETE assessment is usually dependent on the offender's probation officer. In the majority of services referral for ETE assessment is at the discretion of the individual probation officer and is by no means automatic. Of the 11 services visited the exception is Surrey, where *all* offenders are referred to a Community Development Officer for a needs assessment. This includes ETE issues, such as accommodation. This is an effective means of ensuring that all offenders are interviewed in a systematic and consistent way, in the course of which aspects of literacy can be examined routinely. Data derived from ETE assessments of all offenders would be a useful basis for estimating the range and character of literacy needs within a population of offenders, and for planning (including the financing) of appropriate intervention.

Methods of screening were inconsistent and in many cases uninformed. In the majority of the services visited there was no attempt to gather evidence on all offenders as they became known to probation officers in order to select individuals upon whom more detailed assessments needed to be carried out. Where routine screening was attempted this tended to focus on a particular client group, such as unemployed offenders.

More typically a few probation officers had developed their own strategies for checking on some aspects of some offenders' literacy or numeracy. Some officers rely on intuitive hunches; others pick up clues from offenders ('Can you help me write for a job?'); some ask the offender to perform a simple task (e.g. to read from a newspaper). These are examples of the 'proxy' measures outlined above. In Somerset and until very recently in Surrey some probation officers were given copies of a dyslexia checklist which was sometimes, but not always, used with offenders. In the ILPS at Woolwich and broadly across Lewisham screening for dyslexia was carried out by education tutors. However, none of the probation officers knew whether the indicators were valid or reliable, or knew how to interpret the results. In Wiltshire a screening instrument has been developed, but individual probation officers choose whether or not to use it. This includes giving a piece of text to an offender and asking questions to check reading comprehension.

Knowledge of offenders' educational backgrounds

Probation officers generally did not have access to information from schools relating to the educational experiences or achievements of young offenders. Such information can, we recognise, be hard to come by. Probation officers were often unfamiliar with the school provision in the areas in which they worked and so were unable to tell from an offender's school history whether for example he/she had attended a special school. In only one instance (Swindon) did we hear of an educational development manager consulting an educational psychologist about a young offender. Probation officers also expressed concern about the confidentiality aspects of seeking information from other agencies about offenders' educational backgrounds without first seeking the offender's permission. The fact that in general they did not seek that permission presumably reflects the low priority accorded to educational issues.

Information from prison records

Some offenders have been subject to detailed assessments of their educational needs during prison sentences. Information on the educational profiles of offenders with prison records did not generally seem to be either accessible or consulted. In any event there is no certainty that ex-prisoners have been screened or assessed for educational difficulties.

Referral for more detailed educational assessment

A very few probation officers use formal testing. Exceptions include the occasional use of an adult dyslexia profile (ILPS, Nottingham, Somerset, Surrey). Probation officers generally are not able to answer questions about the validity or reliability of any assessments they carry out, including tests for dyslexia. There is some evidence of collaboration with educational psychologists and dyslexia organisations (e.g. Surrey Literacy Project, 1995: a partnership with the West Surrey Dyslexic Aid Association). However it may be helpful to note at this point that there is a distinction to be made between dyslexia and generic literacy difficulties. Individuals may have low levels of literacy competence due to poor school attendance, lack of interest or motivation, or the failure of a school to provide appropriate teaching. In contrast, some individuals, despite good ability levels, motivation and school attendance, struggle with aspects of literacy because of an underlying specific deficit such as perceptual or motor organisation fault or a problem in recalling word sequences.

Many probation officers expressed the view that literacy and its assessment are specialist areas which they have neither the training nor the experience to carry out. We would agree that detailed, formal assessment is the province of the specialist. This is not to underestimate the important role which probation officers have in the initial screening and referral of offenders for such assessments.

In Surrey all probation officers must refer all offenders to the Community Partnership Development Team for ETE assessment, although literacy is only one aspect of this and depends on offenders' self-report. In Somerset, by contrast, referral is encouraged as service policy, but left up to the individual officer to decide. Over most of the services visited referral was on the Somerset pattern.

Documentation

The lack of any standard documentation reflects the somewhat haphazard approach to referral outlined above. Documentation is important because it allows a profile of individual competencies to be built up over time, which then permits a bridge between agencies. It also enables a service to keep track of what has been done for an individual and to provide a basis for summarising the broad needs of the offender population.

There is little consistency across services over *when* documentation is raised, *what* is recorded, and what *function* this is intended to serve. We found no standard format for documenting literacy needs; often we found no documentation specific to literacy at all. In Leicestershire, for example, at the pre-sentence report stage 'education and training' issues are rated numerically alongside eight other issues ('accommodation', 'employment and unemployment', 'financial', 'relationships', 'health', 'alcohol', 'drugs' and 'leisure') on a scale of priority from 0 to 4. This pre-sentence report monitoring form is an attempt to ensure that all relevant issues are covered when a report is prepared for the court. It is no more than an *aide-memoire;* it does not provide a detailed account of educational needs. The pre-sentence report appears to be the main form of documentation employed in the referral process, even at the stage of assessment and identification of problems by ETE officers.

There is also wide variation within services. For example, Oldham district uses an 'Education, Training, Employment and Leisure' assessment. However, in other parts of the Greater Manchester Probation Service this document is not used. In Mid-Glamorgan, at the initial supervision plan stage, 'education' is one of five core issues (alongside 'employment', 'alcohol and drugs', 'accommodation', and 'money matters'). Space is allocated on the form for the probation officer to indicate whether this is a critical issue for the offender concerned, whether it will contribute to further offending, and what action should be taken. One of the functions of the plan is to suggest specific interventions: individual casework; referral to a groupwork programme; referral to other agencies; and so on. Even though there may be a service-wide pro-forma which requires boxes to be ticked signifying that education needs have been considered, it is left very much up to the individual officer to decide what evidence to draw on when considering education needs, and to make his or her own judgement as to whether these needs are critical.

Probation officer reluctance to refer

Evidence from all services visited indicates that the central issue which determines access to literacy help is probation officer referral. There are probation officers in most services who *never* refer offenders for literacy help. Referral practice is inconsistent, depending on awareness of literacy issues and priority given to this. Many probation officers are far more concerned with pressing social problems such as a lack of accommodation, debt, or addiction than with how far the offender's lack of literacy competence has been a component in creating these difficulties. A second reason for non-referral is lack of knowledge concerning how to screen literacy competence in offenders. A third difficulty is that many probation officers are unsure how to present or 'sell' the issue of literacy to offenders, motivating them to address this aspect of their lives. Most probation officers believe that literacy (as part of education) matters, but they are uncertain about the relevance of literacy to their work with offenders. Offenders are considered by many probation officers to be reluctant to disclose literacy difficulties and perhaps skilful at concealment. It follows that officers generally prefer to focus upon what they conceive to be more pressing or less embarrassing matters.

There is also a confidence issue. Most probation officers feel confident in making complex judgements about offenders, for example in assessing risk of re-offending. In our view this is no less difficult, given appropriate training, than screening offenders for literacy needs. Techniques of eliciting information from offenders' histories, reviewing past experience, collating information from other sources, are similar to the techniques employed when screening literacy. However many probation officers interviewed expressed a lack of confidence both in screening and in projecting literacy positively to offenders. They will require additional training to gain the confidence to do this. This could be addressed during initial training and incorporated in the competencies expected of all probation officers, although if immediate progress is to be made the provision of appropriate in-service training is probably even more significant.

Offender reluctance

There are particular problems for young offenders, close to their school experience, in addressing issues which are associated with largely negative experiences of school. Even when needs have been identified they may be reluctant to accept help. The thought of having to go to a strange place which resembles school can lead an offender to reject the provision, even having made a commitment. The availability of in-house provision can help to overcome this problem, although probation officers may be reluctant to waste colleagues' time by referring offenders who in the past have not turned up for appointments. Some officers are reluctant to introduce offenders to too many agencies, especially where any new relationship creates anxiety.

Concluding comments

We observed how varied and incomplete the referral process is in practice. No service even begins to approach the consistency and scope of the framework we outlined at the beginning of this section. Given that the success of literacy support relies on efficient referral, it is doubtful whether the educational needs of offenders will be adequately identified, never mind catered for, under the present arrangements. It is also very unlikely that the services of outside tutors are being used effectively. This is very poor use of a key resource and so deserves to be tackled for that reason alone, although our more fundamental concern lies with the present lack of awareness of the central role of literacy in establishing social competence in offenders.

The nature of literacy intervention

As with staffing and organisational arrangements, the nature of literacy intervention also varies widely between services, and there may be several different kinds of provision on offer. The types of provision reported can be characterised as:

Table 3.2: The Nature of Literacy Intervention

Type	Definition	Example
A Basic Skills Class	• A group of learners, taught Basic Skills as a whole class.	• Community-based classes in Community Schools (open to all age-groups). • College of Further Education • Leicestershire Partnership Agency refers offenders to this provision
An Education Group	• A group of learners receiving a *range* of educational support (not simply Basic Skills). This includes both small–group and individual tutelage, usually involving an Individual Learning Plan	• Often to be found in a Day centre, or a Probation Centre. • Usually held in a resource room on the premises of the probation service. • Swindon and Gloucester Probation Centres are excellent examples of this type of provision.

Figure 3.2: The nature of literacy intervention cont.

Type	Definition	Example
Drop-in Group	• The provision may share premises with other groups in partnership. An Adult Education tutor waits at a pre-appointed time for offenders to 'drop in' for assistance	• Often to be found in a Day Centre, or a Probation Centre. • The tutor tends to be mobile, providing and carrying resources. • Cheltenham, Mid-Glamorgan, and Surrey operate a system of this type
One-to-One Tutoring	• This provision relies on pre-arranged appointments between a tutor and offender. • Individual Learning Plans are negotiated by the tutor and the learner and reviewed on a weekly basis	• Depends where the tutor is located, so could be in a Probation Centre or on the premises of the partnership agency, or (rarely) through a home-tutoring arrangement as in Gloucestershire. • *Making Headway* - Cleveland Partnership Agency and *Crossroads Project* in Woolwich each operate an interesting example of this provision.
Groupwork Support	• Offenders with learning difficulties identified before, or during programmes of groupwork (e.g. *Challenging Offending Behaviour*) are helped during groupwork sessions by one person (usually a volunteer, sometimes a sessional assistant).	• Takes place wherever the groupwork programmes are happening (usually a Probation Centre). • Bridge Street Probation Centre in Oldham and the Squire Lucas Probation Centre in Leicester each operate an interesting example of this provision.

Achieving qualifications

While the nature of the work undertaken by offenders within services varies greatly, many are working towards qualifications such as *Wordpower* and *Numberpower.* These are achieved through the accreditation of offenders' work within distinct modules. This modular arrangement frees both offenders and tutors from the need to follow a prescribed syllabus within time limitations. Several providers endorsed these qualifications, referring to the motivation which results as offenders gain both a certificate and a stepping stone towards other studies. One service (Swindon Probation Centre) also assists students in working towards GCSEs.

A literacy curriculum

Literacy tuition in probation services is mainly characterised by optional 'drop in' encounters with adult education tutors who work in one-to-one or small group settings on skill-based programmes which are unconnected to the other rehabilitation work of the probation service. Furthermore it exists with one foot in probation day centres and one foot on the premises of adult education centres. There is one instance (Oldham) where literacy tutors, ETE officers and probation officers work together on an integrated curriculum. This involves jointly planning the content of programmes to address both rehabilitation and educational attainment; developing resources together; sharing programme delivery; and identifying those areas of rehabilitation which can be supported by literacy work. For example, a 'Motor Vehicle Offenders Programme' is introduced using written resources and driving documentation. Exercises involve 'reading the road' (i.e. thinking through the 'literacy' of driving) as offenders discuss the meaning of road signs and the conventions of safe driving. Attendees are prepared for the written test which is now part of the driving test. This is a particularly fine (although rare) example of probation officers making links between the social and educational needs of their clients. A curriculum with such an integration of social and educational elements offers an exciting prospect for the future.

Monitoring and evaluation

By *evaluation* we mean the methods used to determine the effectiveness of the provision. By *monitoring* we mean the mechanisms used to describe what is happening (e.g inspection). In the absence of national guidance for literacy provision it is up to individual services to set their own criteria and to devise, carry out and monitor this provision as they see fit. We have already noted that provision for literacy is idiosyncratic and erratic. This is also characteristic of evaluation and monitoring.

Reporting back to the probation service (not case specific)

There was little evidence the services visited have developed quality assurance mechanisms in this area of work, beyond recording the number of offenders attending and completing courses. In the few instances in which good quality provision has developed there is always a history of collaboration with adult education managers in the locality. Such collaboration invariably pre-dates Circular 40/94.

The move towards partnership has involved a restructuring of resources and provision: most services are beginning their action plans on a three-year basis. It is likely that the more long-standing collaborations have established strategies to sustain quality as a result of having to defend their existing provision, whereas new developments have yet to determine the means by which quality is assured. In the case of service level partnerships, there is a written agreement which amongst other things will generally cover expected outcomes and how these will be measured. Some of those interviewed could not identify specific outcome measures (not having the documentation to hand). In general it appears that the providers make written and oral reports at intervals to individuals and groups within the probation service, outlining their success in meeting performance targets. For example, *Making Headway* in Middlesbrough provides monthly reports to the probation service (and other funding bodies). The partnership agreement at Oldham requires the project worker to conduct monthly reviews with the local SPO, to provide progress reports at bi-monthly steering committee meetings, and to submit a full written report annually.

When the provision is organised *within* the service (which may include the deployment of external resources such as FE college tutors, volunteers or sessional assistants), evaluation depends on existing systems used to evaluate the work of service personnel, examples being monthly meetings with line managers and/or team meetings. Thus in Swindon no separate formal evaluation of the provision is undertaken and objectives are set as part of the service's annual target-setting exercise. At Nottingham annual reports are made to the probation service by the manager of what was formerly the BEAVER Project (now the Practical Assessment Team). Literacy is but one part of this project and so is only a part of what is being evaluated.

The measures used tend to be quantitative in nature. For example in Leicester the service level agreement specifies the number of clients to be referred to the agency and the number of clients to be seen. Reports to the probation service include information concerning subsequent placements, for example into employment, training, voluntary work or further education. The Cleveland partnership agency *Making Headway* employs similar outcomes. Even when the evaluation is less formalised (usually when the provision is organised from within, such as at Swindon and Gloucester) data will be supplied which cover number of referrals, attendances and completions, and employment taken up. Areas with a history of literacy provision (Swindon and Woolwich are good examples) argue forcefully for sensitive *qualitative* measures of educational attainment as well as *quantitative* measures ('bums on seats' in common parlance). One exception to the emphasis upon quantitative indicators is at Oldham where the partnership agency is evaluated using ALBSU (now BSA) National Standards in addition to a variety of quantitative performance indicators.

Provider evaluation of individual offender progress

Information concerning individual progress is not formally reported back to the probation service in the same way as are quantitative measures of the provision as a whole. Nonetheless all providers have an evaluative framework of some kind in place. This typically involves the setting of flexible goals and learning plans in negotiation with the student for a specified period of time. This could range from a one-hour session to several weeks, depending on the type of provision.

Types of goals, plans and means of measurement vary according to the type of provision. A sessional tutor in Somerset who works with students on a casual basis sets goals with the student at the beginning of the session which are orally reviewed at the end by tutor and student, with both keeping a record of the session. In services such as Oldham, Cleveland, Gloucester, Swindon, Mid Glamorgan and Avon, tutors encourage students to use the work that they have done to gain qualifications, for example *Wordpower.* The evaluation process includes measuring student achievement in the various units. In general, whatever the type of provision, those delivering literacy services adopt accepted practices such as goal setting, action planning and regular feedback with the student. This is part and parcel of their own educational practice rather than something specifically required by the probation service.

While the information on individual students is not fed back to the probation service in a formal way, many of those interviewed made contact with the student's PO to keep him or her informed of the student's progress and, whilst seeking not to disclose confidential information without securing the student's permission, would discuss specific problems or issues. This information may then be considered in the context of the offender's overall supervision plan. For example, an offender may have been placed on an employment programme which is inappropriate because it requires literacy levels which are beyond him/her. It was suggested to us that informal contact with POs was important in promoting the value of literacy work so that further referrals were more likely to be made.

Provider evaluation of literacy provision as a whole

Literacy providers employed by the probation service are usually subject to the annual setting of performance targets of which literacy may be one element. Meetings with line managers may also be held but these are usually to discuss specific cases and ongoing issues. When a group of people is involved with the delivery of a service, such as in Gloucester and Swindon, team targets may be set. Supervision for probation service volunteers and sessional assistants is inconsistent, ranging from that described above to no appraisal at all.

Supervision of those employed outside the probation service is also highly variable. Partnership agencies such as *Making Headway* in Middlesbrough have clear job descriptions for their tutors who have both a monthly supervision meeting with the manager and bi-monthly team meetings. Evaluation of FE college tutors varies according to the type of provision. A tutor from GLOSCAT who teaches at a probation centre undertakes regular meetings with a local ETE officer and is also subject to the appraisal system of his college. In contrast, the FE tutor providing a 'drop-in' facility for Mid Glamorgan probation service attends probation service team meetings but has experienced a lack of a consistently applied individual appraisal or team meetings at her college since a recent change in management.

Student feedback is the other main form of internal evaluation. Providers claim to encourage feedback about their service and to ask for suggestions for improvement. Some providers such as at Oldham use exit questionnaires and interviews as part of the overall evaluation of a given programme. Questionnaires are also used at *Making Headway* in Middlesbrough, but as the tutor there pointed out, the completion of questionnaires requires the offender to display a level of literacy which many students do not possess. Consequently tutors may have to assist the student with the completion of the questionnaire, thereby bringing the reliability of the results into question.

In addition to the ongoing evaluative processes described above, one provider has been conducting longitudinal research into the effectiveness of its provision. The BEAVER project in Nottingham began in 1977, since which time records of the number of participants have been maintained, including details of literacy and job readiness upon entry to and exit from the programme. These figures have provided the basis for annual reports to the probation service. Two follow-up studies of programme participants have also been undertaken by independent organisations. At present a senior manager in the probation service (who was responsible for the creation of the project) is preparing a report of the findings from data gathered over the life of the project.

Probation service monitoring of literacy provision

Monitoring of provision by the probation service appears to rely on the (broadly quantitative) information supplied by the provider. Services take on trust the quality of the provision, although they may have very limited opportunity to observe tutoring even where this is provided on probation service premises. There is also the possibility of some informal student feedback to POs and ETE officers (or equivalent). A number of those interviewed were open about their reliance on the systems used by providers, noting that 'they' (for example, colleges) are the 'experts' and therefore must be presumed to know what they are doing.

Literacy work undertaken on probation service premises can be monitored by observation by probation service staff, but this does not appear to be undertaken in a formalised way. One partnership organisation, *APEX Leicestershire*, noted that their staff are unable to visit and observe all the classes to which offenders may be referred. Recognising their reliance on the evaluative mechanisms of other organisations, APEX told us they make contact with those organisations and investigate their quality control systems before they refer offenders. They additionally keep in contact with students throughout their programme to see how they are progressing and to plan follow up action (such as entry to another course or assistance with job seeking).

External monitoring

Gloucester and Wiltshire reported having been visited in 1988 as part of a Home Office inspection of education provision. However, apart from the inspection of files and paperwork in the course of other Home Office inspections, none of the providers could recall their literacy work being scrutinised in any depth. The Oldham and Swindon informants were however anticipating a Home Office visit to inspect the implementation of Circular 40/94.

The Swindon probation centre and the Youth Education Service in Avon have each invited and undergone inspection by the Basic Skills Agency by whom they were awarded the quality mark. This included observation of tutoring, interviews with tutors and students, and inspection of all planning, teaching and administrative documentation. While these two services were the only ones visited who reported undergoing formal inspection by the BSA, many identified it as an advisory body alongside organisations such as Bridgebuilders, The National Institute of Adult Continuing Education (NIACE), and various Adult Education Groups. All services visited stressed the value of these organisations in providing guidance on both the development of literacy provision and its formal evaluation.

4 The future

Certain themes can be identified in our informants' predictions of the future of literacy within probation. First is the emphasis placed on partnerships, mentioned by 23 senior managers and 12 of the more directly implicated staff. Most saw a *reduced* direct role for their service in literacy provision, with a corresponding increase in the use of partnership agencies. For many this development was acceptable because of the greater level of expertise available. But partnerships were also viewed with caution in some quarters. The 'processing' of offenders by organisations which did not recognise their particular needs was viewed with unease, and there was also concern that literacy might drop to the bottom of some external agencies' agendas. Partnerships were disliked by a few because they were seen as symptomatic of the 'shrinking' of the work of the probation service. Moreover the work involved in setting up partnerships was seen to be time-consuming and difficult to fund. One manager highlighted the short-term nature of some partnerships and the need to have an exit strategy in place. Even so, the dominant view was that partnerships were a way, perhaps the only way, to bring about an expansion in literacy provision, provided arrangements could be made which suited offenders.

It is perhaps significant in relation to this last point that while partnerships were seen as the way of the future, 15 of our informants mentioned that they would expect such arrangements to be supported by in-house provision, generally in terms of more effective identification of literacy problems by probation officers and, secondly, by the pre-course preparation of offenders.

Eight informants commented on the need to change service culture and motivate probation officers to assess and refer offenders with literacy problems. Two of these were senior managers who were particularly critical of officers' lack of awareness of the problem. They saw the need for a cultural change in order to promote referrals and encourage literacy work generally. Six services identified the need for more research in order to prove the need for literacy intervention, to define the nature of provision, and to enable its effectiveness to be judged.

Nine senior managers and six of the more directly involved staff drew attention to the problem of funding. Literacy provision was said to be "hanging by a thread" by one manager. Another said that her service could not afford to do very much about literacy, and one ETE specialist described literacy as 'a luxury the probation service cannot afford'. The probation service could not, in the view of these informants, do everything that was desirable in meeting offenders' needs and would require extra resourcing if literacy was to become a focus of future work. Two senior managers told us bluntly that literacy should not be part of probation practice. On the other hand, almost half (46%) of our probation service informants said that they would wish to see more provision, more flexibly organised, and with an element of in-house provision which in their view would help to improve take-up. We were told by five services that they had just introduced, or were about to introduce, literacy projects or new procedures.

To sum up, the overall impression to be drawn from probation service perspectives on the future of literacy provision is that additional concentration on this area is desirable, but is hampered by uncertain funding and a lack of a clear understanding as to the place of literacy within probation work. Furthermore there is a perception that central government's emphasis upon the punitiveness of community penalties is inconsistent with or does not encourage a focus upon offenders' literacy needs.

We shall now attempt to identify some of the steps which could be taken to enhance aspects of literacy provision, bearing in mind the differences in starting points between services. Wherever possible we identify a range of strategies which reflect these contrasts. We also make recommendations which could be implemented at a national level, for example in relation to policy guidelines.

Why literacy should be a priority in the future

We have promoted a view of literacy as a social practice, best taught and developed in relation to specific purposes such as the writing of a letter seeking a job or rent rebate, or the reading of a technical manual in order to operate a piece of equipment. There is a growing consensus that literacy is an important component in every individual's ability to deal with day-to-day transactions. There are very few contexts which do not have a literacy component. It follows, therefore, that most literacy practices can be promoted with reference to offenders' ability to manage personal circumstances. Given that probation officers see their role as helping offenders to change their social practices, to address their offending behaviour, and to keep within the boundaries of the law, then the ability to address literacy needs should be an important component of the probation officer's professional armoury.

National Policy Guidelines

A major issue facing probation services is to determine the part that literacy should play within their professional role. Priorities in probation service work reflect policy guidelines and the advice of professional bodies. The Association of Chief Officers of Probation (ACOP) could provide guidance, through its Training Committee, on the place of literacy work within probation practice. It would also be helpful for probation services to have clear statements from the Home Office on:

- how literacy may be defined more broadly in relation to offenders' personal organisation, social responsibility and reintegration

- the role of the probation service in screening for literacy needs, referring offenders for detailed ETE assessment, and securing and evaluating literacy provision

- literacy intervention as an integral part of rehabilitative programmes.

Training issues for probation officers

Few probation officers whom we interviewed could recall having addressed literacy issues within their initial training. In most instances this had reflected social work traditions. Relevant knowledge from an educational perspective had not been central to that training. In future it is likely that probation committees will be able to recruit from a wider range of applicants. Area probation services are likely to be funded to meet their own training requirements, with prospective probation officers recruited as salaried trainees. Training arrangements are likely to become more flexible and practice-orientated, tailored to prior qualifications and previous experience, and modular in format.

Whatever the eventual form of initial training for entry to the profession, coverage of literacy issues should be a component of all training routes. This should make explicit the place of literacy work in securing the rehabilitation of offenders. It should also include relevant practical skills. Specifically, we believe that all probation officers should be able to undertake initial screening of literacy difficulties. Ideally, training should give experience in the use of screening instruments and in interview techniques geared to eliciting information about offenders' educational histories. These practical skills should then be included in the core competencies required of all probation officers.

The role of higher education institutions

The training and development needs of probation service personnel should prompt local institutions of higher education to engage in a dialogue with probation services managers. Some higher education institutions might develop a range of accreditable modules with a literacy focus aimed specifically at probation services.

The continued professional development of existing probation staff will also need to be addressed. Here too there is scope for the introduction of courses with a literacy focus, leading to further professional qualifications.

Developing a local service view of literacy

The research undertaken demonstrates that probation services do not have a clear, consistent or openly discussed view of literacy. This in turn leads to wide variations in the extent to which literacy needs are screened, identified and planned for. With a few exceptions the question of whether an offender's literacy needs are addressed is a matter of chance, reflecting the personal interest and enthusiasm of a few probation officers. It is important for all services to have an overview of what they currently provide in terms of literacy intervention; a policy which identifies specific objectives and theoretical underpinnings; and a plan of action which sets targets and time scales. For services at different starting points, we would suggest the action plan shown in figure 4.1

Figure 4.1: Developing an action plan

No provision	A service could:
	• Identify a senior manager, ETE officer, and Adult Education specialist • Provide them with a short-term brief to explore the implementation of literacy support within the service • Set up a small steering group to draft policy which defines literacy and the place of literacy in probation work • Use a professional development day to raise awareness of literacy issues and discuss the policy draft
Emergent provision	A service could:
	• Review job descriptions for all probation officers and seek the inclusion of statements of general expectations regarding literacy screening and referral • Review job descriptions for senior managers and seek the inclusion of specific responsibilities regarding the management of literacy screening and referral • Use a professional development day to explore opportunities for the inclusion of literacy practices within groupwork sessions • Gather examples of successful practice in groupwork to share across the service • Begin to formalise a groupwork curriculum which emphasises literacy development as part of the process of rehabilitation
Mature provision	A service could:
	• Map out a full policy review cycle to review strengths and weaknesses over a three-year period • Implement a system of appraisal which includes issues of literacy awareness, screening, referral, planning and intervention, with specific opportunities for professional development • Develop recognised and accreditable post-professional training • Establish a network of consultants and 'literacy experts' who are available to provide input to the service

Determining the extent of need

It is impossible to plan appropriate resources at either local or national level without effective methods of determining the extent of need. Simply stated: we have no measure of the extent of the problem of low literacy levels amongst offenders under probation supervision. There is an absence of hard data, with services unable to quantify, or even approximate, numbers of offenders with literacy needs on their caseloads. We would suggest measures shown in Figure 4.2.

Figure 4.2: Measuring need

No provision	A service could: • Ask selected/all members of probation teams to go through caseloads and try to identify at least one client who might have an educational need • Employ a tutor to make a fuller assessment • Pilot a feasibility study and/or needs analysis for a cohort of offenders • Use such data and feedback as a way of gauging how many other offenders are likely to require assessment and intervention
Emergent provision	A service could: • Carry out service-wide review of those probation officers who have never referred offenders for educational support • Devise a standard format/system for ensuring that every offender has had at least some attention paid to educational need • Document educational plans and outcomes
Mature provision	A service could • Refer all offenders for a more detailed ETE assessment • Define levels of need in the population known to the service • Evaluate the appropriateness of current provision in meeting the spectrum of needs, and adjust accordingly

Organisation of provision

It is clear from the research data that existing provision for literacy varies widely in nature, quality and scope from one area to the next. In most areas provision is not organised or allocated on a coherent and systematic basis. The research data also indicate that services struggle to know how to evaluate the effectiveness of any interventions which are organised and so are not best placed to plan future provision.

Figure 4.3: Organising provision

No provision	A service could: • Appoint a SPO with a specific brief for the professional development of colleagues in relation to literacy • Review methods of screening and referral • Explore contacts and contracts with tutors • Explore involvement with existing providers in the community such as: FE colleges, Adult Education programmes, and recognised charitable organisations • Contact the Basic Skills Agency for advice concerning material provision: premises and resources • Note that there is likely to be least difficulty in sustaining offender involvement when support is given on probation premises
Emergent provision	A service could: • Extend the range of alternatives: drop-in schemes; in-house provision with tutors employed directly; group programmes; and external providers • Establish clearer definitions of the role of tutors, volunteers, sessional assistants and ETE officers by reviewing job descriptions and performance indicators • Secure tutors' involvement in probation service meetings and use their expertise through formal consultancy arrangements • Co-ordinate timetables and publish schemes of work • Involve tutors and assistants in developing measures to evaluate the effectiveness of their literacy work

Contd.

Figure 4.3: Organising provision contd.

Mature provision	A service could: • Evaluate the effectiveness of different arrangements for different offenders by considering drop-out rates, re-offending, and which schemes achieve qualifications • Provide professional development for all personnel, leading to qualifications such as City Guilds 9282/9285 • Ensure that partnerships are entered into only following a careful audit of clients' needs • Pilot partnerships before fixing contracts • Conduct a full literacy audit and publish a report to attract further funding • Co-opt, educate and involve local magistrates in the maintenance of educational provision

The nature of provision

As with staffing and organisation, our research indicates that the character of literacy intervention varies greatly. We would expect this variety of intervention to continue until such time as national guidelines are made explicit.

Figure 4.4 : Developing provision

No provision	A service could: • Identify those offenders with very limited literacy competence • Use established Adult Literacy programmes, probably as one-to-one support • Employ a qualified and experienced Adult Education tutor who should work in the following ways: 1. organising and providing basic skills teaching, preferably at a probation centre 2. working alongside probation officers to assist in screening and developing learning plans for offenders with the most immediate educational needs 3. collaborating with a SPO to plan the integration of literacy support within groupwork 4. collaborating with an ETE officer to establish partnerships with an educational focus
Emergent provision	A service could, in addition to the above: • Define and select one or two opportunities to begin to integrate literacy issues in groupwork sessions • Consider team-teaching, with probation officers and tutors planning activities and designing resources together • Develop and sustain collaborations between probation officers and tutors
Mature provision	A service could • Ensure regular opportunities for all probation officers to work with literacy tutors • Re-examine existing rehabilitation programmes and plan further ways of integrating literacy work across practice • Create links with other community organisations – for example, schools, youth centres, social services departments and local police – to engage youth currently known to be at risk of exclusion or on the brink of persistent offending behaviour

Referral routes

The research data indicate that none of the services visited has a comprehensive framework for screening, assessment and action planning which is applied to all offenders. Given the importance of the referral process in ensuring that offenders have access to literacy support, these issues are crucial.

Figure 4.5: Planning a referral system

No provision	A service could:
	• Establish clear lines of communication between probation officers in the field and ETE officers • Spell out screening and referral procedures in policy documents • Arrange short term monitoring so that all probation officers list the names of offenders referred and note perceived difficulties in making referrals
Emergent provision	A service could • Introduce service-wide documentation systems, consistently applied • Request a regular report on implementation and success rates by an Assistant Chief Probation Officer • Seek feedback on the working of the referral system from a range of users: offenders, volunteers, tutors, probation officers, ETE personnel
Mature provision	A service could • Refer all offenders for ETE assessment • Establish educational portfolios for all offenders, in which individual provision is documented, attainments are recorded and achievements are celebrated • Establish in-house research partnerships in order to explore and validate new systems of referral and methods of integrated literacy support • Share practice nationally and internationally through journals, conferences and other publications • Become a centre of excellence, thereby contributing to further professional development regionally and nationally

Finally

Many of the above suggestions have been drawn from current practice, or were suggested to us by the personnel whom we interviewed. We are convinced that change will be welcomed if it is supported and guided from the top and if it is seen to enhance and support the work of the probation service as a whole.

Appendix 1

Area summaries

We now present seven area summaries:

- Greater Manchester

- Wiltshire

- Surrey

- Gloucestershire

- Nottinghamshire

- Leicestershire

- Cleveland

Whilst we visited 11 areas in total, we consider that the accounts of literacy work in these seven areas are sufficient to give an accurate sense of the range of provision. All the main organisational arrangements and forms of engagement with literacy problems are represented here in summary form. As will be seen, we make no claim to provide a comprehensive account of provision within each area; we are typically referring to work carried out in just one centre. This will commonly represent the pinnacle of that service's engagement with literacy work.

Figure A1.1 Greater Manchester area summary

Where?	When?	Why?	Who
Oldham Rhodes Centre	25–26 April 1996	• Metropolitan • North–West England • Oualtiy Reputation • Prior Invitation • Useful 'benchmark' for pilot study	• SPO • PO (Day Centre) • Education Co-ordinator • Basic Skills Curriculum Leader • PSO • Sessional Worker • Offender • Offender

Research Focus

Oldham is one of ten areas within the Greater Manchester Probation service (GMPS). We were 'directed' to Oldham because of its innovative developments. While the literacy provision at Oldham is not representative of provision throughout GMPS, we were informed that two other areas are beginning to follow Oldham's lead. The provision described below refers only to the work carried out at the Rhodes Day Centre. We were not introduced to, and so have made no attempt to describe, other ETE work in Oldham or Greater Manchester as a whole.

History

The unique feature of the Oldham project is the integrated nature of the work undertaken by the self employed Education Co-ordinator (who is herself the partnership organisation), the *Oldham Youth and Community Education Service* (OYCES), and probation service staff at the Rhodes Day Centre. This has developed over the past three years. Prior to April 1993 five hours per week of basic skills teaching (of which literacy was a major component) was delivered for offenders at the day centre by Oldham Community Education (now OYCES). It was realised by both parties (probation and OYCES) that common goals and values underpinned their work as both are concerned to help individuals develop skills and practices that would enhance their ability to cope with everyday life. Consequently the parties met to explore ways in which they could integrate their activities. A 10-week block of basic skills teaching was delivered by the OYCES Curriculum Leader to pilot new teaching techniques and initial basic skills assessment for offenders who requested it. This led to a successful bid to ALBSU to fund a six month project which aimed to: integrate basic skills into the day centre programmes (Motor Vehicle Offenders, Employment, and the Offence Focus), undertake educational assessments (Basic Skills) for offenders, provide City & Guilds 9282 Initial Certificate training for staff, and raise the profile of Basic Skills within the Oldham Probation Service. Following what was deemed to be the success of this initiative it was decided to continue the work of the project since when various means of funding have been deployed to ensure its continuance (see below).

Main organisational features

The provision is managed by a team comprising the Head of the OYCES, the day centre SPO, delegated POs, and the OYCES Curriculum Leader. The ongoing organisation and delivery of the provision is undertaken by the Education Co-ordinator (project worker) and the SPO in collaboration with the OYCES Curriculum Leader. Training and accreditation for City & Guilds 9282 *Initial Certificate in Teaching Basic Communication Skills* is provided for probation staff by the Education Co-ordinator and OYCES.

Offenders access the provision through one of the following: referral for Education, Training, Employment and Leisure assessment (ETEL) by their supervising PO; self referral; or attendance at one of the probation centre's core programmes (such as the programme for Motor Vehicle Offenders) which is usually attended by offenders on a probation order with a condition to attend the centre; or through attendance at voluntary classes such as craft or cookery. The ETEL assessment was designed by the education and employment staff in consultation with the Careers Service and contains an initial literacy and numeracy assessment which has been adapted from Basic Skills Agency (BSA) assessment materials. The assessment is carried out at the probation centre by City & Guilds 9282 trained sessional assistants, the SPO and the Education Co-ordinator. If appropriate the Education Co-ordinator will undertake a more in-depth literacy and numeracy assessment.

Sessional assistants, volunteers and probation officers work alongside students in the day centre groups (such as the Motor Vehicle Offenders programme) to help them achieve competencies as defined by BSA National Standards. Basic Skills teaching resources (of which literacy forms a major part) have been adapted to facilitate students' achievement of City & Guilds

Wordpower and Numberpower qualifications. Literacy and numeracy groups are run as part of the day centre programme. The Education Co-ordinator works closely with the SPO, reports bi-monthly to the steering committee, and submits an annual written report.

The provision is currently funded from within the GMPS partnership budget under the title of the Open Links Education Project. It is a partnership between the service and the former project worker (Education Co-ordinator) who is now defined for partnership purposes as an independent organisation. She uses partnership funds to pay herself, employ tutors and administrative assistants, and meet the cost of accreditation fees. OYCES contributes through providing tutors, staff and volunteer training, clerical assistance, student accreditation, educational support, and placements and further education opportunities for students. OYCES is funded by the Local Educational Authority (LEA) and the Further Education Funding Council (FEFC). The probation service provides office space, heating, lighting and a telephone.

Philosophy and practice

The success of this provision rests on an agreed view of the role and place of basic skills within the work of the probation service. The organisation and planning of the project has also required a large amount of time and effort from key organisers. The aims of the project have been met without compromising the statutory content and objectives of the programmes. Staff at all levels in the day centre are committed to the integration of basic skills into the programmes. This has meant a significant level of extra professional development, including City & Guilds 9282 training. All those interviewed talked about the importance of team work and their reliance on each other. Each demonstrated a real understanding of the need for literacy work to be pursued in context.

This provision is an excellent example of how literacy work can be undertaken in the context of programmes which have meaning for participants, rather than being taught as an isolated set of skills.

Figure A1.2 Wiltshire area summary

Where?	When?	Why?	Who?

Swindon
 	
Swindon
Probation
Centre
	5-6
	May 1996
		• Rural with dense
		  conurbation
		
		• South-West England
		
		• Quality reputation
		
		• History of literacy
		  provisin
			• PO Probation Centre
			
			• Education Co-ordinator
			
			• Assistant Education
			  Co-ordinator
			
			• Jobwise Consultant
			  (ETE equivalent)
			
			• Offender
			
			• Offender

Research Focus

Although we only visited the Swindon day centre, this being now the primary educational provision, the Education Co-ordinator at Swindon was able to provide us with a county wide account.

History

The Education Co-ordinator has been employed by the Wiltshire probation service since 1981, her brief being to develop educational provision for Wiltshire probation service. The Education Unit was initially financed for one year by NACRO and the Wiltshire probation service. Thereafter funding was provided jointly by the Wiltshire probation service (who paid the Education Co-ordinator's salary and provided premises) and Swindon College who provided a tutor to work at the Unit. The tutor believed in 'student centred learning' which for him meant having a completely unstructured programme. As this approach was deemed inappropriate for the student group (offenders) his services were dispensed with, following which the College reduced their tutorial support to two mornings per week. To bridge the gap the probation service employed a full time tutor to assist the Education Co-ordinator in teaching the classes and in developing the work of the Unit. The Unit continued until 1989 to provide classes five mornings a week, recruiting students from across the county. This was a county-wide service in that the Education Co-ordinator also taught a weekly ABE class at Salisbury and organised and supported classes at Trowbridge and Chippenham.

The Co-ordinator had found the experience of developing the Unit very isolating as there was no support within the probation service for those working in education. She was contacted by staff from Kent who were in similar roles and a meeting was organised to share experience and ideas. As a result of these meetings the organisation *Bridgebuilders* was formed with the aim of providing support for those working in education within the probation service.

In 1991 the Education Unit became part of the Swindon probation centre programme. This was related to the need for centre staff to deliver the Reasoning and Rehabilitation programme which had recently been introduced, and also because of perceived under-utilisation of the Education Unit. The Education Co-ordinator and her assistant (who reduced her hours from fulltime to .5) took on responsibility for delivering some of the R and R modules (such as Social Skills) for the day centre programme. Education classes were reduced to two sessions per week, one of which was made compulsory for those attending the probation centre whilst the other was voluntary.

As a result of the Education Unit being incorporated into the probation centre, equal access to educational provision for offenders across Wiltshire was lost. The Education Co-ordinators' responsibility for county wide provision was removed because the time taken up with delivering R and R programmes in addition to the education classes meant that it was no longer possible to meet educational needs outside Swindon. Only the Chippenham ABE class, which was funded by the probation service and run by a tutor from Chippenham College, continued. This class is now funded through the ETE partnership *Jobwise* (see below) which has responsibility for educational provision outside the Swindon area.

Main organisational features

Most offenders attend the education group as part of the 12-week programme run at the Swindon day centre for offenders who are subject to a court order to attend (the current programme is 42 days over 12 weeks). A few offenders attend on a voluntary basis but this is not common. Voluntary attendees can be referred either by their supervising PO or by an ETE worker. The ETE workers are from *Jobwise,* an independent organisation operating in financial partnership with the Wiltshire probation service to provide ETE services. The precursor of *Jobwise* was an Employment/Training/Education Officer funded by the Employment Service. The funding for this post was then briefly taken over by Wiltshire Probation Service before the independent organisation *Jobwise* was created to provide ETE services to Wiltshire Probation Service through partnership. The former

ETEO became the co-ordinator of *Jobwise.*

Initial ETE screening is supposed to be carried out by each supervising PO. This covers employment, training and educational needs, including basic skills. All offenders who are unemployed, unhappy with their current employment, or who wish to pursue further training or education should be referred to the ETE officer for in-depth assessment (unless there are factors which preclude employment, training or education). POs have at their disposal a screening tool for literacy and numeracy skills. If literacy needs are identified the offender will be referred directly to the Education Co-ordinator. It is up to individual POs to decide whether to use this tool and some may still refer to the provision without using it. The ETE assessment includes discussion of educational needs and our ETE informant noted that this sometimes results in the identification of literacy needs which have been missed by the PO. Consequently some offenders may be referred to the education provision following ETE assessment.

Offenders subject to a court order to attend the day centre undertake one compulsory education session per week as part of that programme. Each offender is assessed by the Education Co-ordinator prior to the start of the programme. Assessment lasts for around 30 minutes and involves discussion of educational experiences and aspirations. It may include the completion of various literacy tasks, depending upon the student's current skill levels. Tuition is provided by the Education Co-ordinator, her .5 assistant, a .2 college tutor and six probation service volunteers who each work between 2.5–5 hours weekly. Both the Education Co-ordinator and her assistant had extensive teaching experience prior to their employment by the probation service. Both hold the RSA Diploma in Teaching and Learning in Adult Basic Education. Volunteers are required to undertake training to achieve the City & Guilds 9282 Initial Certificate, the fees for which are paid by the probation service. Staff are continuing to develop skills (such as computer skills) to meet changing student needs. In addition to the tutoring, the Co-ordinator and her assistant assess potential students and are involved in the delivery of other probation centre programmes.

Students negotiate a 12-week individualised programme of activities. Individual and small group tuition takes place four hours per week in a comprehensively resourced classroom. Students work on individual learning programmes with tutor support and also undertake independent learning activities which are designed to allow them to proceed independently of the tutor. Progress is reviewed on a monthly basis. Students are encouraged to work towards a range of qualifications ranging from City & Guilds qualifications such as Wordpower to secondary school qualifications such as GCSEs. Short courses are also being developed by the permanent staff in order to address specific needs such as computer skills.

The work of the Unit is promoted to magistrates in an effort to help them understand offenders' educational needs and see how the Unit is attempting to meet these. Magistrates' evenings are held in the classroom at the day centre so that first hand knowledge can be gained of the way in which students are assessed and the types of learning plans negotiated. The classroom is set up with a range of materials and activities on display to demonstrate the nature of the activities that students undertake. The potential benefits of the provision are outlined, including the actual cost of day centre attendance compared with custody. These evenings are also supported by other probation centre staff and the ETE worker from *Jobwise*.

Philosophy and practice

The Education Co-ordinator expressed concern about the gradual reduction of educational provision across the county and in Swindon since the incorporation of the Education Unit into the day centre in 1991. She believes that the 1.5 fulltime educationalists (her and her assistant) are not deployed in the most effective way by the service, as evidenced by the fact that there is only four hours of education provision because of the demands of the other probation centre work. She argues that without someone to co-ordinate and promote countywide provision the number of referrals will drop and classes will not be sustained. Voluntary referral to the Swindon classes was more easily encouraged when the provision was housed on the same premises as one of the supervision teams. This is reflected in the fact that voluntary referrals have increased since the Under 21 Team moved into the day centre building.

Also of concern to the co-ordinator was the emphasis on the number of offenders gaining employment and the use of successful employment placements as a key performance indicator for the ETE service. She argued there is a lack of attention paid to offenders' educational achievement and that progess will not be made until there is a recognition from senior management that education is important for offenders. This suggested lack of commitment was evidenced by the lesser status afforded to educationalists throughout the service, as illustrated by the fact that they are usually classified as probation service officers and are on a lower pay scale than probation officers even though many hold equivalent qualifications. There is also a lack of specific training for educationalists working with offenders. This is now being rectified by NACRO and City & Guilds who are creating special courses.

The Education Co-ordinator at Swindon has with her assistant developed a service which is an excellent example a quality educational provision delivered alongside other groupwork activities to form a probation centre programme.

Figure A1.3 Surrey area summary

Where?	When?	Why?	Who?
Woking Guildford	9–10 May 1996	• London/South–East commuter belt • Wealthy conurbation with pockets of poverty • Emphasis on dyslexia testing • History of local initiative	• Community Partnership Development Team: • Manager • CPD Officer • CPD Officer • PO • Offender

Research Focus

While our visit was centred at Woking and Guildford Day Centres, one of our informants, the Development Manager, is responsible for the implementation of the county wide employment strategy which includes literacy provision. Our account therefore includes an outline of provision throughout the county.

History

Prior to 1993 literacy assistance for offenders in Surrey had been provided on an *ad hoc* basis. In 1993 two Employment Development Officers were employed by the Surrey Probation Service to develop an employment strategy for the county within the framework of ETE. They developed an ETE referral and assessment procedure named STEP (Steps Toward Employment Programme) which was based on the premise that education and training were important steps towards employment. After the strategy was devised one of the officers left to become the County Training Manager and the other became the Development Manager responsible for implementing the plan. In November 1993 four Community Partnership Development Officers (CPDOs) were recruited through internal advertisement to carry out assessments at the county's four probation day centres.

Prior to March 1996 offenders were referred for ETE assessment at the discretion of their PO. The assessment was designed to identify offenders' employment, training and education needs. This took the form of an interview which included asking offenders about their educational background and confidence in reading and writing. Those identified as having literacy needs were offered support by means of individual tuition from probation service volunteers. The Development Manager began to establish a team of volunteers throughout the county. Team members were encouraged to gain the City & Guilds 9282, with their fees paid by funds from ALBSU and the Further Education Funding Council (FEFC).

Between April 1995 and March 1996, of 781 referrals 195 did not attend. Records were kept of the 586 who undertook assessments, their action plans, and the outcomes in terms of placement into employment, training or education. Approximately 40 per cent gained employment or undertook further training or education. By autumn 1995 the success of those attending for assessment had become evident and as a result the Surrey CPO decided to implement mandatory assessment. It was decided that from March 1996 POs would be obliged to refer all offenders for ETE assessment unless they could make a case otherwise. The assessment was also extended to include accommodation needs.

In addition to the ETE work, in 1994–1995 The Surrey Literacy Project was piloted by the Surrey Probation Service in conjunction with the West Surrey Dyslexic Aid Association. Funded by the JJ Charitable Trust, the Home Office and Surrey Probation Service, the project was initiated by a magistrate who was a member of the West Surrey Dyslexic Aid Association. The project was run in three areas: Guildford probation centre, HMP Send and St Catherine's Hostel. POs and Hostel Officers were trained by an educational psychologist and a special needs teacher to administer a preliminary screening test (Vernon Graded Word Spelling Test) to all offenders in those settings. Offenders with a spelling age of 10 years and under were then given a further test to diagnose the nature of the problem before being offered remedial tuition. Volunteer assistants received training from the educational psychologist and the special needs teacher to administer the second test and provide follow up tuition. The tuition system used was the Wilson Reading System, selected because it was designed to be administered by volunteers rather than literacy specialists and because it was being used in a similar project in Baltimore, USA.

After the project had begun the Development Manager was asked to take over its management. She had reservations about the project (such as the appropriateness of requiring POs to administer tests, and only providing tuition to those who met specific criteria) but felt it provided an opportunity to raise the profile of literacy work. Problems arising from the project included: very few offenders actually scoring a spelling age of 10 or below; a reluctance on the part of POs to use the tool (which was deemed discouraging to offenders); the length of time the test took to administer; and concern about what was to be done with offenders who clearly had literacy problems but scored a spelling age above 10. A number of steps were taken to address these problems, including raising the required spelling age to 12 years. While positive results were reported for the few offenders who received tuition, the project was not continued as it was decided that literacy needs could more appropriately be addressed in the context of the Development Team's assessment work, with referrals made to in-house and external provision as appropriate.

Current organisational features of STEP

Mandatory referral for STEP for all offenders on a probation order in Surrey began on March 1 1996. This initially met with a measure of resistance from some POs who saw it as usurping their role. However, officers became more supportive having seen the benefits to offenders under their supervision.

On referral to STEP offenders undergo assessment in terms of education, training, employment, accommodation and basic skills. Literacy needs are identified as part of the assessment process by asking offenders about their educational background and presenting them with a list of basic skills (such as letter writing, punctuation etc.) with tick boxes labelled: Can do/unsure/ would like help with. On the basis of the needs identified an action plan is negotiated with the offender. The plan is sent back to the supervising officer for approval. STEP assessments are carried out throughout the county by CPD officers (a further four were recruited in January 1996). Two CPD officers are located in each of the four probation centres.

At the time of our visit, if literacy needs were identified through the STEP assessment individual tuition was provided at one of the four probation centres by a tutor from the established group of volunteers. A bid has been made to the Home Office to fund a volunteer co-ordinator who will recruit, train and support volunteer basic skills tutors. It is also proposed to offer individual ABE tuition delivered by tutors from the Adult Youth and Continuing Education Service. It is hoped that by employing tutors from the Adult Youth and Continuing Education Service offenders will feel more comfortable about attending courses run by that organisation. While funding is being sought there is an informal arrangement with the Adult Youth and Continuing Education Service whereby their tutors do work for the probation service on a voluntary basis in Guildford and Woking.

Philosophy and practice

Although literacy issues are addressed within Surrey Probation Service's employment strategy, there is a commitment to addressing the literacy needs of all offenders. This is evident in the inclusion of responsibility for addressing literacy issues within the Development Manager's brief through her management of the Surrey Literacy Project. The Development Manager is now to implement a basic skills self assessment (the STEP assessment) to be administered to all offenders supervised by the service. Surrey was the only service visited where ETE work (including literacy) is supported in this way. Consequently, while Surrey is still in the process of developing its assessment method and its approach to meeting identified needs, of the services visited it is the only one in which offenders' access to literacy support of some kind is almost guaranteed. This has been made possible through Chief Probation Officer support for mandatory assessment.

Figure A1.4 Gloucestershire area summary

Where?	When?	Why?	Who?
Gloucester	23 May 1996	• Rural & small town communities • West of England • History of educational emphasis • County-wide approach	• SPO Partnerships • 3 ETE Officers • Tutor from Gloscat (local college) • PO • Offender • Offender

Research focus

The town of Gloucester is one of three areas within the Gloucestershire probation service which has an ETE officer. The county provision was originally developed by the Gloucester based ETE officer who operates from the Gloucester Barbican Centre which was the site of our visit. Although this was the only site visited, the ETE officers responsible for the Cheltenham and Stroud areas and the SPO with overall responsibility for ETE were jointly interviewed at the Barbican Centre. Consequently we gained an overview of literacy provision in the county as well as a more detailed understanding of the work done at the Barbican.

History

The ETE officer based at the Barbican Day Centre was employed in 1986, originally under the title of 'Educationalist'. A similar post had previously existed within the day centre but it had lain vacant for a considerable period before her appointment. Her brief was to ensure the availability of educational guidance and provision for the Gloucester area (in the first instance) and thereafter across Gloucestershire. Although previous incumbents had established links with adult literacy groups and had operated a referral system, these had to be re-established. Various small group programmes, including some education groups, were established at the centre. Resource and time constraints meant that the same level of provision could not be made available outside the Gloucester area. However, a database of available community provision was compiled for use by POs. The ETE officer visited outlying areas to provide educational and career guidance to offenders on referral from their supervising officer. In 1990 a further two ETE officers were employed part-time to work in the Cheltenham/North Gloucestershire and Stroud/South Gloucestershire areas, with the existing ETE officer covering Gloucester, the Forest of Dean and the Barbican Centre.

Main organisational features

A unique aspect of the Gloucestershire service is that all ETE officers have teaching qualifications and experience. Consequently each can be involved in the delivery of literacy tuition if appropriate. The ETE officers are responsible for developing and maintaining ETE provision (of which literacy is a major part) within their designated area and each works as a member of their area probation team. As a group they are also responsible for county-wide provision in conjunction with a SPO who has recently been given overall responsibility for the ETE team. Prior to this each ETE officer was responsible to a different SPO, which made the development and implementation of a county-wide strategy more problematic.

The majority of offenders are referred to the area ETE officer at the discretion of their supervising officer. Once referred, an action plan is negotiated between the ETE officer and the offender. The ETE officers expressed concern that referral is dependant upon probation officer judgement. There are plans to investigate the possibility of introducing county-wide screening and assessment but there is concern over the increased number of referrals that this is likely to generate and uncertainty as to how additional demand will be met.

Adult Basic Education (including literacy) is provided through individualised learning programmes with variable lengths of attendance. The object is to improve offenders' basic education skills to enable them to develop better coping mechanisms and greater self-esteem so that they become less inclined to reoffend. All these programmes are managed by the offender's area ETE officer. Offenders may undertake a programme on a voluntary basis or as a condition of probation. There are two courses (the eight-week Creative Learning and six-week Work Matters courses) intended for offenders for whom literacy/numeracy or unemployment have been identified as factors in their offending.

Provision across the county varies according to the availability of resources. The Barbican Centre is a county-wide resource with a specially equipped education room. Education groups are held there, as are other programmes (such as Make Your Experience Count). The ETE officer works with a Gloucester College of Art and Technology (GLOSCAT) Basic Skills tutor and probation volunteers to deliver basic skills programmes to students through individual and group tuition. This includes literacy work. This staff group also delivers group guidance on the '1A3' programme (which raises awareness of opportunities in education and training). Work undertaken at the sessions is often in support of other programmes such as college courses and the job club (a service which provides advice about gaining employment, including CV preparation, job seeking, letter writing and interview skills, and provides free use of resources such as a photocopier, fax and computers so that participants can prepare applications). Students often work toward City & Guilds qualifications such as Wordpower and Numberpower. In-house certificates are issued for short courses.

The same level of in-house provision is not available in the rest of the county. However, ETE officers spend considerable time finding places for students on community programmes or in local colleges. Individual tuition is sometimes delivered by volunteers and sometimes by ETE officers themselves in order to help those who are unable to access community provision because of geographical isolation or a lack of confidence. A drop-in scheme run by the ETE officer and a volunteer tutor (who also tutors in a local community centre) is currently being piloted on Cheltenham probation service premises in an effort to provide a stepping stone to community provision for those offenders who have low self-esteem and poor educational experiences. Offenders living in the Forest of Dean and other districts sometimes travel to Gloucester for ABE help.

The ETE officer posts are financed directly by the Gloucestershire probation service. Tutors from organisations outside the probation service who teach on courses are paid by their employer (college or community group). Telephone and photocopying are provided by the probation service. Funding is also provided from other sources including Adult Continuing

Education and Training (ACET), NACRO, The Princes Trust, Southwest Midlands Trust and The Barnwood Trust.

Philosophy and practice

The Gloucestershire probation service has a long-standing commitment to providing education for offenders. Commitment to county-wide educational provision is demonstrated by the initial appointment of an education specialist and subsequent employment of ETE officers with teaching qualifications and experience. Gloucestershire's commitment to county-wide education provision is also evident through the appointment of a SPO with overall responsibility for the team (instead of each ETE officer being responsible to their team SPOs). This reflects a belief that policy could be better developed and implemented if the team answered to one line manager. The ETE team's philosophy of education as a means of helping offenders take control of their lives was evident throughout our interviews. The ETE officers are committed to increased accessibility (through tuition at a probation service site or tutoring at the student's home). They emphasise the importance of helping offenders get to the point where they are equipped to access community provision.

This service shows how the employment of educationally qualified staff can enhance literacy provision and how ETE officers operating in different areas can work together to develop and maintain a coherent approach county-wide.

Table A1.5 Area Summary Nottinghamshire

Where?	When?	Why?	Who?
Nottingham	7 June 1996	• Urban industrial • North Midlands • Home of the BEAVER project	• ACPO • Manager of PAT • PO • Offender

Research Focus

Until recently the literacy provision for Nottinghamshire has been provided in the context of the BEAVER project (see below). Recent restructuring of the service has resulted in the literacy component being offered by the Practical Assessment Team (PAT) whose premises were the main location for our visit.

History

The BEAVER Project began in 1977 and was developed and implemented by the Nottinghamshire Probation Service's current Employment Development Officer. It was set up because of the high rate of unemployment among offenders, this being attributed to a lack of job readiness due to poor basic skills. The aim of the project was to give offenders the opportunity to have their skills levels (including literacy) assessed in the context of practical activities (initially woodworking, later extended to photography and pottery) and then to prepare for work by developing their skills through an individualised 60-day programme.

The project was initially funded for two years by Home Office project money (which targeted the assessment of offenders in bail hostels) and was then extended for a further two years on condition that the Nottinghamshire Probation Service would continue to fund the project after Home Office funds ceased. The project was initially staffed by a manager, a woodwork instructor (whose role grew to include trainee assessment), a basic skills tutor funded by the local FE college, a secretary, and a part-time van driver/store person. By 1989 the staff had grown to include four Employment Officers and a PSO who was responsible for liaising with offenders released from prison on a temporary release scheme.

Offenders were referred to the project by their supervising probation officer, attendance being voluntary. (The project also accepted offenders under a temporary prison release scheme and it took some students, all long-term unemployed, who were not offenders.) Participants undertook a five-day practical assessment through a variety of workshop activities. It was felt this provided an opportunity to assess participants, actual abilities rather than relying on self reports to probation officers, these having been found to be inaccurate once offenders were placed in employment.

Literacy was assessed throughout the five days by observing and assessing trainees' reading and writing in the context of the practical work being undertaken (e.g. following instructions on how to develop a film). On the basis of the assessment a contract was drawn up in the form of an action plan which gave 60 days of BEAVER support. Small group tuition was provided as part of this, delivered on the premises by a Basic Skills tutor from Clarendon College (tuition was originally piloted on College premises close to the service but attendance was almost nil–due, it was thought, to offenders' low confidence levels). The tutor worked with students on individual programmes tailored to the practical work being undertaken.

The work of the BEAVER Project has been evaluated by Nottingham and Manchester Universities. The Nottingham University study involved follow-up interviews with former trainees two years after they had completed the programme. Fifty per cent reported that the programme had improved their confidence, social skills and employability. The Manchester University study developed a reconviction prediction measure based on an existing Home Office tool. Criminal records information was used to compare the *actual* reconviction rate of former trainees with the predicted reconviction rate. The actual reconviction rate was found to be significantly lower than the predicted rate. The findings from these independent studies and the trainee information systematically collected over the life of the project have provided the basis for a report currently being prepared by the service's Employment Development Officer.

In 1989 a decision was made by the Nottinghamshire Service to continue funding BEAVER as a means of addressing ETE issues. After Circular 40/94 this was reviewed and five ETE officers (four from partnership organisations, see below) were deployed to service the county's probation teams. Following funding cuts in 1995 the BEAVER project was reduced in scope. Some of the workshop activity has been redistributed to the Community Service Team. The assessment and skills development work (which includes literacy) has been reduced and is now undertaken under the auspices of the recently formed Practical Assessment Team (PAT). PAT is the BEAVER project in a substantially reduced form.

Current organisational features

The Practical Assessment Team is currently staffed by a Manager, two Employment Development Officers (on temporary one-year contracts), two part-time secretaries, one volunteer basic skills tutor and one volunteer. The PAT currently run a modified version of the original five-day practical assessment over two days (including literacy). They also run a five-day job preparation course, a job club, and have drop-in sessions to provide offenders with the opportunity to carry on their skills development in the absence of the 60 days support which is no longer available. The job club and job preparation course are staffed by a partnership project, *Jobs Opportunities In Nottingham* (JOIN). Funding for JOIN comes from the Training Enterprise Council and the European Social Fund.

Until September 1995 literacy tuition used to be delivered by a Basic Skills tutor from Clarendon College. However, recent changes in FE funding criteria have resulted in the loss of this tutor. Further education funding is now based on the number of students who attend classes and this requires a minimum of 8–10 students to attend regularly. The PAT were unable to meet this criteria, having lost a number of students in the course of restructuring and moving (they moved venues twice in three months). The PAT manager is very aware of the problems offenders face in attending provision in the community and is determined to build up student numbers to the point where they meet the new criteria so that tuition by the college tutor can resume.

In the interim literacy support is provided on probation premises by a Basic Skills volunteer tutor acquired through Volunteers In Probation (VIP) who receive funding from the Nottinghamshire Probation Service and operate from the Nottingham Council of Voluntary Services. The volunteer provides individual and group tuition to students, engaging them in activity related to the work they are doing with the PAT or which is of personal interest to them.

Offenders are referred to the PAT project by ETE officers. Field team POs put forward clients for assessment by an ETE officer on the premises where the offender attends supervision sessions. The assessment takes the form of a one hour interview during which education, training and employment needs are discussed. There are five ETE officers, only one of whom (the PAT manager) is funded entirely by the probation service. The others are employed by multi-funded partnership projects: Inside Out; Offenders Probation Employment Network (OPEN); and Offender Employment Information Service (OEIS). These projects are funded by North Nottingham TEC, Greater Nottingham TEC, European Social Fund, Single Regeneration Budget (European funding), City Challenge, and the Nottinghamshire Probation service. These partnerships have grown from various probation service project initiatives. It is part of the Employment Development Officer's role to secure funding for them.

A jointly funded project with the Dyslexia Institute is being piloted at the PAT. Offenders who are identified by ETE officers and field POs as possibly dyslexic as defined by the Dyslexia Institute (as distinct from having an undefined learning problem) are offered the opportunity of assessment by the Institute tutor. If found to be dyslexic they are offered a programme of assistance. ETE officers and POs (one from each field team) were asked to attend a training day run by the Institute. This was designed to inform staff about dyslexia and show them how to apply the screening tool. This project was instigated through the interest of a field team PO and the PAT manager.

There are also plans to re-establish a project (HOPE) in which ETE type assessments (including literacy) were undertaken at the PSR stage with a target group of burglars scheduled to appear in Crown Court and therefore at high risk of custodial sentences. From this assessment an ETE report was written and submitted for consideration by the court alongside the PSR, the purpose of this being to identify needs which could be better met by a community rather than a custodial sentence. As a result of the project there was calculated to be a 24 per cent increase in the number of offenders who received community sentences. The original project was funded by the Home Office for three years from 1991–1994. Plans are now afoot to seek funds to run a similar project in 1997.

Philosophy and practice

Literacy provision in this service has traditionally been embedded within programmes which aim to help offenders gain worthwhile employment. Recent funding cuts have resulted in the loss of the established in-house literacy provision and although a volunteer is being deployed in the interim the intention is to secure FE funding so that tuition by the college tutor can resume. The integration of literacy assessment within practical activities reflects the emphasis placed upon offender interests and susceptibilities, especially the fears harboured as a result of negative educational experiences.

Table A1.6 Leicestershire area summary

Where?	When?	Why?	Who?
Leicester	6 June 1996	• Urban multi-ethnic communities • North Midlands • Self report of 'very little' provision	• ACPO • SPO Day Centre • • Apex Adviser • 3 POs • SPO (Prison) • Offender

Research focus

Prior to their involvement in this study Leicestershire Probation Service lacked a unified approach to addressing offenders' literacy needs. As a consequence of their participation in the postal survey a decision was made to rectify this. The SPO ('Development Officer') who manages the Squire Lucas Day Centre (where the visit was based) is now responsible for the development of literacy provision at the day centre with a view to expansion across the service.

History

The Squire Lucas Day Centre was founded in 1979 and was one of the first to be established in England. Various programmes have been run at the centre, including in-house literacy tutoring by an Adult Basic Education tutor, funded by the LEA from 1980–1993. Changes in FE funding meant that this tutor was lost to the probation service. It appeared that take up was poor, due it was thought to the stigma attached to admitting to having literacy difficulties. For offenders not attending the day centre, literacy needs would be addressed if identified by the supervising officer. He/she would refer directly to community provision or, for ETE assessment, to APEX Leicester Project Ltd.

Main organisational features

It is currently up to individual POs to identify offenders having literacy difficulties when interviewing them at the PSR stage or in the course of supervision. Referral is either made direct to an Adult Basic Education provision such as a Community College (particularly for offenders living outside Leicester) or to APEX Leicester Project Ltd through whom the probation service primarily address wider ETE issues, particularly employment.

Originally part of the national charity by the same name, APEX Leicester Ltd became an independent charitable organisation in 1982. The aim of the organisation is to work with all ex-offenders in Leicestershire (and offenders in custody) to help them gain worthwhile employment, training or further education. It runs two job clubs for offenders, one of which (St Nicholas) offers a Computer Literacy and Information Technology course delivered by a qualified tutor. APEX has formed links with educational providers and employers throughout the county. It also provides advice regarding the content of the programmes run at the day centre. It employs a Project Director, two Employment Advisers, a part-time Policy Consultant and an

Administrative Assistant. The Management Committee comprises the Project Director and representatives of local business and voluntary organisations. Although APEX is based in Leicester, a county-wide service is provided by its team of advisers who travel to probation service districts outside Leicester. Work with offenders in custody is undertaken by an organisation which is subcontracted to APEX.

On referral to APEX, offenders are interviewed by one of two qualified advisers who, in the context of employment issues, assess literacy levels by gaining details of offenders' educational history and by observing the way in which 'paper work' is handled. If literacy needs are identified, offenders are referred to Adult Basic Education classes within the community. The referring probation officer is kept informed of action taken and made aware of any literacy difficulties identified.

The APEX adviser whom we interviewed emphasised the problems associated with client reluctance to attend both the APEX assessment and community based provision. This was attributed to lack of confidence and poor educational experiences. The advisers encourage POs to accompany offenders to their ETE interview. Tutors taking the ABE classes are informed of students' expected arrival so that appropriate induction can be provided. APEX maintain contact with students as they progress through their course so that follow up action can be planned.

Funding for APEX comes from probation service partnership money, some Home Office money, and the Employment Service who fund the job clubs. The Service Level Agreement between APEX and the Leicestershire Probation Service outlines expectations of the number of referrals to be made by the service, the number of offenders to be interviewed, and offender placement outcomes (in terms of places in employment, training, further education and voluntary work). The adviser interviewed noted that POs are supposed to refer all unemployed offenders. However this does not always happen. There are regular informal meetings between APEX staff and the Development Officer, his line manager (ACPO) and the APEX Project Director. The Development Officer and the ACPO also attend APEX Management Committee Meetings. Formal evaluation of the service is through written reports from APEX. Officers newly appointed to the Leicestershire Service visit APEX as part of their induction to enable them to understand the role of the organisation.

In addition to the ETE work carried out through the APEX partnership, literacy issues are addressed in the context of two day centre programmes. Offenders attending the day centre, either on referral from their probation officer or as a condition of a probation order are asked about their current literacy levels. Those with literacy difficulties are offered the support of a volunteer to work alongside them throughout the course to assist them with activities which are beyond their current capabilities. The day centre also runs two Sex Offenders Programmes, one of which includes an element designed specifically for those identified by a Health Authority Psychologist as having psychologically based learning difficulties. Four POs with a special interest in this area regularly help in the delivery of this programme.

The Day Centre Manager has initiated a project with Derby College Wilmorton and APEX Leicester called the Adult Basic Education Project. This will begin in August 1996 and will initially be for day centre clients. The objectives include establishing a screening system and a diagnostic assessment which will be used to create a learning plan for each student. The hope is that students will work towards a qualification such as City & Guilds Wordpower.

Philosophy and practice

The Leicestershire Service is an example of a service in a relatively early stage of development as far as literacy work is concerned. Their self report of 'doing very little' is not entirely accurate given the evidence of literacy support within two day centre programmes and referral of offenders to community provision either directly by POs or through APEX. It is more a case of having some provision which has come about as a result of the somewhat uncoordinated efforts of individuals within the service rather than as a consequence of a service level decision to address literacy issues.

The issues faced in the development of this service's provision highlight the need for national guidelines to assist services in developing, implementing, evaluating and funding an appropriate literacy provision from a low base.

Table A1.7 Cleveland area summary

Where?	When?	Why?	Who?
Middles-brough	20 June 1996	• Urban industrial	• SPO
		• North–East England	• Manager–Making
		• High unemployment	• Tutor – Making Headway
		• Small Service	• PO
			• Offender

Research focus

Cleveland probation service has been restructured recently. Our visit centred on the Partnerships Unit which is responsible for all probation service links with outside organisations. Literacy support is provided through *Making Headway* and the HOPE project (see below), both of which address literacy in the context of employment issues. We describe the work carried out by *Making Headway*. However we were informed that the HOPE project, which works with Hartlepool offenders, provides a similar service.

History

Between 1978 and 1990 the local educational authority provided the probation service with an Adult Basic Education tutor. In 1993 *Making Headway* was begun, funded by the Cleveland probation service, Cleveland Action Team, Safer Cities, Teeside TEC, Task Force, City Challenge and Employment Services. The intention was to create a job club for which purpose a project worker was employed by the probation service for one year. Once appointed the project worker interviewed a number of offenders to identify the specific problems they faced in gaining employment. From this she decided that a job club approach was inappropriate and that a structured modular programme should be designed to address the identified issues (such as disclosure of convictions, low self-esteem, poor letter writing skills). The aim of the programme was to enable offenders to access existing mainstream services such as the Employment Service Job Club and educational providers.

The modular programme was implemented in October 1993. Problems were soon encountered when the project worker found that one in three of her clients had literacy problems and were therefore unable to undertake parts of the modular programme. Individual literacy and numeracy tuition (with encouragement towards achieving qualifications) was added to the programme and delivered by a volunteer with teaching experience and qualifications. The project was initially staffed by the project worker (by then the project manager), a project assistant and seven volunteers (six general and one for literacy). In the first year the project's target of working with 200 offenders was easily achieved, a total of 543 offenders actually attending the project.

At the end of the 1994 it was decided that the project should continue but should be managed by NACRO rather than the probation service. This arrangement relieved the Cleveland probation service of administrative responsibilities and enabled the project to apply to a greater range of organisations for funding. NACRO provides an administrative service which includes payment of salaries. It receives a fee of 12 per cent of the project's total funding. *Making Headway* has been funded by a variety of organisations since 1994. The current funders are the Cleveland Probation Service (from the partnership budget), Teeside TEC, and the Stockton and Thornaby Task Force.

Making Headway has grown substantially since 1993. Although the organisation is administered by NACRO it is managed by the original probation service project worker who has been assisted by a deputy manager since 1995 (this person began as a volunteer on the original project). The project also employs three full-time tutors and four sessional staff and has a team of volunteers. In addition to the services provided at *Making Headway*'s Middlesbrough premises six outreach programmes have been established to provide a similar service to clients in outlying areas who find it difficult or are reluctant to attend the central service. These are run by the manager with the help of volunteers from the area in which the outreach post is located. The majority of the work, however, is carried out on the Middlesbrough site.

Offenders are referred to *Making Headway* by POs. Officers are encouraged to make telephone referrals in the presence of the offender and to accompany him/her to the initial briefing session. This initial support is seen as vital by the *Making Headway* staff who acknowledge the difficulties associated with being located off probation service premises. Probation service and *Making Headway* informants noted a discrepancy between the number of referrals made and the number attending. However once offenders have actually been to the project they usually decide to attend regularly.

Briefing sessions for groups of referred offenders are held to explain the work of the organisation and expectations of participants. Offenders then decide whether they wish to take advantage of the service. If they decide to proceed an action plan is drawn up based on their educational and employment histories. The employment related modules available include personal development, communication, disclosure (of convictions to employers), and negotiating skills. Action plans for literacy support are determined through individual assessments with literacy tutors. Literacy support is provided through individual and workshop sessions. These are taught by the deputy manager, permanent tutors, sessional workers and volunteers, all of whom hold or are working towards appropriate teaching qualifications. Students work on individual programmes designed in negotiation with the tutor. They are actively encouraged to work towards City & Guilds qualifications. Ongoing support is also provided for students undertaking FE college courses.

Staff attend a monthly supervision meeting with the manager, and regular meetings are held with all staff to review progress and plan future developments. The overall work of the organisation is evaluated through the achievement of outcomes as agreed by the Service Level Agreement (including number of attendances, work completed, and placement in employment, training, education or voluntary work). The manager of *Making Headway* provides a monthly written report to the probation service. Regular meetings are also held with the SPO in charge of the partnership. There is also informal liaison between *Making Headway* staff and probation officers to discuss student progress.

Philosophy and practice

Making Headway is the only partnership organisation visited which provides its own literacy provision as part of its ETE work for the probation service. While the literacy support is provided within the context of other ETE work, the way in which it is provided demonstrates an understanding of literacy needs. This partnership is an interesting example of the development of a special project initiated by the probation service which then grew into an independent organisation working in financial partnership with the service.

Appendix 2

Research instruments

The research instruments employed in the study were as follows:

1. Postal questionnaire sent to all probation areas.

2. Template for semi-structured telephone interviews with (a) ACPO or other senior manager; (b) key internal provider; and (c) external provider.

3. Template for site visit interviews with (a) 'policy officer'; (b) 'supervisory officer'; and (c) offender.

LITERACY AND PROBATION PROJECT

A PROBATION SERVICE SURVEY

IDENTIFICATION

1. What procedures exist in your Service for identifying offenders with literacy problems? (Attach relevant documentation if preferred.)

2. Do the same procedures exist for offenders released from prison and now under your supervision?

3. How does your Service monitor or evaluate the effectiveness of these procedures? (Attach relevant documentation if preferred.)

SCOPE OF LITERACY PROBLEMS

1. How does your Service record (or estimate) the number of offenders with literacy problems?

2. Approximately how many offenders – both in number **and** as a percentage of the offenders being supervised by your Service – received help with literacy problems during the last 12 months?

SUPERVISION AND LITERACY PROBLEMS

1. How does your Service take into account the literacy problems of offenders when they participate in offending behaviour programmes?

2. How does your Service take into account the literacy problems of offenders when they participate in activities concerned with other aspects of re-integration?

3. To what extent has your Service investigated the effect of literacy problems on risk of re-offending?

PROVISION OF LITERACY TEACHING

1. What provision does your Service make, alone or in connection with another organisation, for literacy teaching?

2. How are offenders with literacy problems referred for teaching?

3. How is the effectiveness of literacy teaching provision assessed? (Attach relevant documentation if preferred.)

FOLLOW-UP

Please identify those Probation Service staff, including yourself, who may have responsibility for literacy work or have special expertise in the area and who may be contacted and interviewed by telephone:

NAME & TITLE	WORK ADDRESS	TELEPHONE NO.

Self:

Other(s):

If use is made of another organisation in the provision of literacy teaching, please name a person in that organisation who may be contacted for permission to conduct a telephone interview:

NAME & TITLE	WORK ADDRESS	TELEPHONE NO.

The completed questionnaire should be returned to:
Literacy and Probation Project
School for Policy Studies
University of Bristol
8 Woodland Road
Bristol BS8 1TN

ACPO/Policy Officer

Preamble:
Thanks.
Questionnaire helpful.
This is follow-up call – 15-20 minutes.
Check:
a) speaking to the right person
b) area of knowledge/responsibility
c) who can provide budgetary information
d) they can afford time to talk now.

Have questionnaire to hand for cross-reference
Go over any problems with written questionnaire: pick up
omissions, clarify ambiguities, ask if there is anything significant
missed or important to add.

1. CURRENT POLICY ON LITERACY PROVISION

a) Why does your service provide the level of literacy support that you do, if any?
b) Why this particular type of provision?
c) How important is literacy in terms of the work you do?

2. EVALUATION (check with questionnaire)

What attempt is there to evaluate:
a) the effectiveness of literacy provision overall?
b) individual progress?
c) whether literacy provision is helpful or otherwise to the main work of your service?

3. FINANCE

a) What percentage of your annual budget is allocated to literacy provision?
b) What would be the effect of cut-backs (2%, 5%, 10%) on literacy provision?

4. HISTORY/FUTURE OF LITERACY PROVISION

a) How long has literacy provision been in its current form?
b) Do you think this level of provision is sufficient? Why?
c) What was provided before? What caused this change?
d) What do you see happening in the future? Why?
e) What would you like to see happening in the future?

Key Internal Provider

Preamble:

Thanks.

Questionnaire helpful.

This is follow-up call – 15-20 minutes.

Check:

    a) speaking to the right person

    b) area of knowledge/responsibility

    c) who can provide budgetary information

    d) they can afford time to talk now.

Have questionnaire to hand for cross-reference

Go over any problems with written questionnaire: pick up omissions, clarify ambiguities, ask if there is anything significant missed or important to add.

1. LITERACY PROVISION

What literacy work do you do?

    a) How you see 'the problem' of literacy?

    b) What are your objectives?

    c) Who is involved in your literacy work? (professionals, volunteers – trained/untrained)

    d) Why are <u>you</u> involved to the level you are?

2. THE CLIENTS

    a) How severe are offenders' literacy problems?

    b) How important is literacy to offenders? Why?

    c) If take-up is poor, why?

    d) Are literacy programmes completed? If not, why?

3. EVALUATION (check with questionnaire)

What attempt is there to evaluate:

    a) the effectiveness of literacy provision overall?

    b) individual progress?

    c) whether literacy provision is helpful or otherwise to the main work of your service?

4. FUTURE OF LITERACY PROVISION

    a) What do you see happening in the future? Why?

    b) What would you like to see happening in the future?

Key External Provider

Preamble:

>Thanks.
>
>Questionnaire helpful.
>
>This is follow-up call – 15-20 minutes.
>
>Check:
>
>>a) speaking to the right person
>>
>>b) area of knowledge/responsibility
>>
>>c) who can provide budgetary information
>>
>>d) they can afford time to talk now.

Have questionnaire to hand for cross-reference

Go over any problems with written questionnaire: pick up omissions, clarify ambiguities, ask if there is anything significant missed or important to add.

1. LITERACY PROVISION

What literacy work do you do?

>a) How you see 'the problem' of literacy?
>
>b) What are your objectives?
>
>c) How are you financed?
>
>d) Who are your staff? (professionals, volunteers – trained/untrained)

2. LINKS WITH THE PROBATION SERVICE

What are the links with probation service in terms of:

>a) cash transfers?
>
>b) referrals – who? how?

3. THE CLIENTS

>a) How severe are offenders' literacy problems?
>
>b) How important is literacy to offenders? Why?
>
>c) If take-up is poor, why?
>
>d) Are literacy programmes completed? If not, why?

4. EVALUATION (check with questionnaire)

What attempt is there to evaluate:

>a) the effectiveness of literacy provision overall?
>
>b) individual progress?

Policy Officer: CPO, ACPO, PO, ETEO

Service:_____ **Participant/role:** _____

Date: _____ **Interviewer:** _____

Tape Details: _____

background	policy: • national expectations • local decisions • briefs
experience	implementations: • costing • personnel • schemes
effect	evaluation: • advisory bodies • appraisal mechanisms • performance indicators
growth	evolution: • research • reconnaissance • training • conference

Policy Officer: CPO, ACPO, PO, ETEO

Service: _____   **Participant/role:** _____

Date: _____   **Interviewer:** _____

Tape Details: _____

background	initial training: • qualification • appropriateness • areas of competence
experience	employment: • previous • job description • briefs • practices
effect	appraisal: • inspection • team review • references
growth	development: • initiatives • courses • specialisms • mentorship

Policy Officer: CPO, ACPO, PO, ETEO

Service: _____ **Participant/role:** _____
Date: _____ **Interviewer:** _____
Tape Details:_____

background	circumstances: • nurture •significant adults • literact access
experience	education: • consequences • rapport • ambition
effect	reflection: • motivation • compliance • plans
growth	rehabilitation • efforts • setbacks • resolutions

References

ALBSU (1994), *Basic Skills in Prison: Assessing the Need,* London: The Basic Skills Unit.

Barnes, C., Hollin, C.R., and Martin, G., (1984), *Changes in Young Offender Scores Over Time on Measures of Intelligence and Literacy,* Directorate of Psychological Services Report, Series II, No. 130, London: The Home Office.

Home Office (1988), *Punishment, Custody and the Community,* Cm. 424, London: HMSO.

Home Office (1990), *Partnership in Dealing with Offenders in the Community: A Discussion Paper,* London: HMSO.

Home Office (1991), *The Criminal Justice Act 1991,* Chapter 53, London: HMSO.

Home Office (1992), *Partnership in Dealing with Offenders in the Community: A Decision Document,* London: Home Office.

Home Office (1994), *Employment, Training and Education Guidance for the Probation Service,* Probation Circular No. 40, London: The Home Office.

Home Office (1995a), *National Standards for the Supervision of Offenders in the Community,* London: HMSO.

Home Office (1995b), *Strengthening Punishment in the Community: A Consultation Document,* London: HMSO.

Palmer, E.J., and Hollin, C.R., (1995), *Education and Work Programmes in Prisons: Effect on Recidivism. A Report for the Planning Group,* HM Prison Service, University of Birmingham.

Porporino, F.J., and Robinson, D., (1992), *Can Educating Adult Offenders Counteract Recidivism?* A report prepared for the ACA Winter Conference, Portland, Oregon, Correctional Service of Canada.

Roberts, K., Barton, A., Buchanan, J., and Goldson, B., (1996), *Evaluation of a Home Office Initiative to help Offenders into Employment,* A Report for the Home Office Research and Statistics Directorate, London: Home Office.

Stewart, G., and Stewart, J., (1993), *Social Circumstances of Younger Offenders Under Supervision,* A Research Report for the Association of Chief Officers of Probation, London: ACOP.

Walmsley, R., Howard, L., and White, S., (1991) *The National Prison Survey 1991: Main Findings,* Home Office Research Study 128, London: HMSO.

Publications

List of research publications

A list of research reports for the last three years is provided below. A **full** list of publications is available on request from the Research and Statistics Directorate Information and Publications Group.

Home Office Research Studies (HORS)

133. **Intensive Probation in England and Wales: an evaluation.** George Mair, Charles Lloyd, Claire Nee and Rae Sibbett. 1994. xiv + 143pp. (0 11 341114 6).

134. **Contacts between Police and Public: findings from the 1992 British Crime Survey.** Wesley G Skogan. 1995. ix + 93pp. (0 11 341115 4).

135. **Policing low-level disorder: Police use of Section 5 of the Public Order Act 1986.** David Brown and Tom Ellis. 1994. ix + 69pp. (0 11 341116 2).

136. **Explaining reconviction rates: A critical analysis.** Charles Lloyd, George Mair and Mike Hough. 1995. xiv + 103pp. (0 11 341117 0).

137. **Case Screening by the Crown Prosecution Service: How and why cases are terminated.** Debbie Crisp and David Moxon. 1995. viii + 66pp. (0 11 341137 5).

138. **Public Interest Case Assessment Schemes.** Debbie Crisp, Claire Whittaker and Jessica Harris. 1995. x + 58pp. (0 11 341139 1).

139. **Policing domestic violence in the 1990s.** Sharon Grace. 1995. x + 74pp. (0 11 341140 5).

140. **Young people, victimisation and the police: British Crime Survey findings on experiences and attitudes of 12 to 15 year olds.** Natalie Aye Maung. 1995. xii + 140pp. (0 11 341150 2).

141. **The Settlement of refugees in Britain.** Jenny Carey-Wood, Karen Duke, Valerie Karn and Tony Marshall. 1995. xii + 133pp. (0 11 341145 6).

142. **Vietnamese Refugees since 1982.** Karen Duke and Tony Marshall. 1995. x + 62pp. (0 11 341147 2).

143. **The Parish Special Constables Scheme.** Peter Southgate, Tom Bucke and Carole Byron. 1995. x + 59pp. (1 85893 458 3).

144. **Measuring the Satisfaction of the Courts with the Probation Service.** Chris May. 1995. x + 76pp. (1 85893 483 4).

145. **Young people and crime.** John Graham and Benjamin Bowling. 1995. xv + 142pp. (1 85893 551 2).

146. **Crime against retail and manufacturing premises: findings from the 1994 Commercial Victimisation Survey.** Catriona Mirrlees-Black and Alec Ross. 1995. xi + 110pp. (1 85893 554 7).

147. **Anxiety about crime: findings from the 1994 British Crime Survey.** Michael Hough. 1995. viii + 92pp. (1 85893 553 9).

148. **The ILPS Methadone Prescribing Project.** Rae Sibbitt. 1996. viii + 69pp. (1 85893 485 0).

149. **To scare straight or educate? The British experience of day visits to prison for young people.** Charles Lloyd. 1996. xi + 60pp. (1 85893 570 9).

150. **Predicting reoffending for Discretionary Conditional Release.** John B Copas, Peter Marshall and Roger Tarling. 1996. vii + 49pp. (1 85893 576 8).

151. **Drug misuse declared: results of the 1994 British Crime Survey.** Malcom Ramsay and Andrew Percy. 1996. xv + 131pp. (1 85893 628 4).

152. **An Evaluation of the Introduction and Operation of the Youth Court.** David O'Mahony and Kevin Haines. 1996. viii + 70pp. (1 85893 579 2).

153. **Fitting supervision to offenders: assessment and allocation decisions in the Probation Service.** Ros Burnett. 1996. xi + 99pp. (1 85893 599 7).

154   **Ethnic minorities: victimisation and racial harassment.
        Findings from the 1988 and 1992 British Crime Surveys.** Marian
        Fitzgerald and Chris Hale. 1996. xi + 97pp (1 85893 603 9).

155   **PACE ten years on: a review of research.** David Brown. 1997. xx
        + 281pp. (1 85893 603 9).

156.   **Automatic Conditional Release: the first two years.** Mike
        Maguire, Brigitte Perroud and Peter Raynor. 1996. x + 114pp. (1
        85893 659 4).

157.   **Testing obscenity: an international comparison of laws and
        controls relating to obscene material.** Sharon Grace. 1996. ix +
        46pp. (1 85893 672 1).

158.   **Enforcing community sentences: supervisors' perspectives on
        ensuring compliance and dealing with breach.** Tom Ellis, Carol
        Hedderman and Ed Mortimer. 1996. x + 81pp. (1 85893 691 8).

160.   **Implementing crime prevention schemes in a multi-agency
        setting: aspects of process in the Safer Cities programme.** Mike
        Sutton. 1996. x + 53pp. (1 85893 691 8).

161.   **Reducing criminality among young people: a sample of relevant
        programmes in the United Kingdom.** David Utting. 1997. vi + 122pp. (1
        85893 744 2).

162   **Imprisoned women and mothers.** Dianne Caddle and Debbie Crisp. 1996.
        xiii + 74pp. (1 85893 760 4)

163.   **Curfew orders with electronic monitoring: an evaluation of the first
        twelve months of the trials in Greater Manchester, Norfolk and
        Berkshire, 1995 - 1996.** George Mair and Ed Mortimer. 1996. x + 50pp. (1
        85893 765 5).

165.   **Enforcing financial penalties.** Claire Whittaker and Alan Mackie. 1997. xii +
        58pp. (1 85893 786 8).

166.   **Assessing offenders' needs: assessment scales for the probation
        service.** Rosumund Aubrey and Michael Hough. x + 55pp.(1 85893 799 X).

168. **Managing courts effectively: The reasons for adjournments in magistrates' courts**. Claire Whittaker, Alan Mackie, Ruth Lewis and Nicola Ponikiewski. 1997. x + 37pp. (1 85893 804 X).

Nos 159, 164 and 167 not published yet.

Research and Planning Unit Papers (RPUP)

86. **Drug Education Amongst Teenagers: a 1992 British Crime Survey Analysis**. Lizanne Dowds and Judith Redfern. 1995.

87. **Group 4 Prisoner Escort Service: a survey of customer satisfaction.** Claire Nee. 1994.

88. **Special Considerations: Issues for the Management and Organisation of the Volunteer Police.** Catriona Mirrlees-Black and Carole Byron. 1995.

89. **Self-reported drug misuse in England and Wales: findings from the 1992 British Crime Survey.** Joy Mott and Catriona Mirrlees-Black. 1995.

90. **Improving bail decisions: the bail process project, phase 1.** John Burrows, Paul Henderson and Patricia Morgan. 1995.

91. **Practitioners' views of the Criminal Justice Act: a survey of criminal justice agencies.** George Mair and Chris May. 1995.

92. **Obscene, threatening and other troublesome telephone calls to women in England and Wales: 1982-1992.** Wendy Buck, Michael Chatterton and Ken Pease. 1995.

93. **A survey of the prisoner escort and custody service provided by Group 4 and by Securicor Custodial Services.** Diane Caddle. 1995.

Research Findings

12. **Explaining Reconviction Rates: A Critical Analysis.** Charles Lloyd, George Mair and Mike Hough. 1995.

13. **Equal opportunities and the Fire Service.** Tom Bucke. 1994.

14. **Trends in Crime: Findings from the 1994 British Crime Survey.** Pat Mayhew, Catriona Mirrlees-Black and Natalie Aye Maung. 1994.

15. **Intensive Probation in England and Wales: an evaluation.** George Mair, Charles Lloyd, Claire Nee and Rae Sibbitt. 1995.

16. **The settlement of refugees in Britain.** Jenny Carey-Wood, Karen Duke, Valerie Karn and Tony Marshall. 1995.

17. **Young people, victimisation and the police: British Crime Survey findings on experiences and attitudes of 12- to 15- year-olds.** Natalie Aye Maung.

18. **Vietnamese Refugees since 1982.** Karen Duke and Tony Marshall. 1995.

19. **Supervision of Restricted Patients in the Community.** Suzanne Dell and Adrian Grounds. 1995.

20. **Videotaping children's evidence: an evaluation.** Graham Davies, Clare Wilson, Rebecca Mitchell and John Milsom. 1995.

21. **The mentally disordered and the police.** Graham Robertson, Richard Pearson and Robert Gibb. 1995.

22. **Preparing records of taped interviews.** Andrew Hooke and Jim Knox. 1995.

23. **Obscene, threatening and other troublesome telephone calls to women: Findings from the British Crime Survey.** Wendy Buck, Michael Chatterton and Ken Pease. 1995.

24. **Young people and crime.** John Graham and Ben Bowling. 1995.

25. **Anxiety about crime: Findings from the 1994 British Crime Survey.** Michael Hough. 1995.

26. **Crime against retail premises in 1993.** Catriona Mirrlees-Black and Alec Ross. 1995.

27. **Crime against manufacturing premises in 1993.** Catriona Mirrlees-Black and Alec Ross. 1995.

28. **Policing and the public: findings from the 1994 British Crime Survey.** Tom Bucke. 1995.

29.   **The Child Witness Pack – An Evaluation.** Joyce Plotnikoff and Richard Woolfson. 1995.

30.   **To scare straight or educate? The British experience of day visits to prison for young people.** Charles Lloyd. 1996.

31.   **The ADT drug treatment programme at HMP Downview – a preliminary evaluation.** Elaine Player and Carol Martin. 1996.

32.   **Wolds remand prison – an evaluation.** Keith Bottomley, Adrian James, Emma Clare and Alison Liebling. 1996.

33.   **Drug misuse declared: results of the 1994 British Crime Survey.** Malcolm Ramsay and Andrew Percy. 1996.

34.   **Crack cocaine and drugs-crime careers.** Howard Parker and Tim Bottomley. 1996.

35.   **Imprisonment for fine default.** David Moxon and Claire Whittaker. 1996.

36.   **Fine impositions and enforcement following the Criminal Justice Act 1993.** Elizabeth Charman, Bryan Gibson, Terry Honess and Rod Morgan. 1996.

37.   **Victimisation in prisons.** Ian O'Donnell and Kimmett Edgar. 1996.

38   **Mothers in prison.** Dianne Caddle and Debbie Crisp. 1997.

39.   **Ethnic minorities, victimisation and racial harassment.** Marian Fitzgerald and Chris Hale. 1996.

40.   **Evaluating joint performance management between the police and the Crown Prosecution Service.** Andrew Hooke, Jim Knox and David Portas. 1996.

41.   **Public attitudes to drug-related crime.** Sharon Grace. 1996.

42.   **Domestic burglary schemes in the safer cities programme.** Paul Ekblom, Ho Law and Mike Sutton. 1996.

43.   **Pakistani women's experience of domestic violence in Great Britain.** Salma Choudry. 1996.

44.   **Witnesses with learning disabilities**. Andrew Sanders, Jane Creaton, Sophia Bird and Leanne Weber. 1997.

45.   **Does treating sex offenders reduce reoffending?** Carol Hedderman and Darren sugg. 1996.

46.   **Re-education programmes for violent men - an evaluation.** Russell Dobash, Rebecca Emerson Dobash, Kate Cavanagh and Ruth Lewis. 1996.

47.   **Sentencing without a pre-sentence report**. Nigel Charles, Claire Whittaker and Caroline Ball. 1997.

48   **Magistrates' views of the probation service.** Chris May. 1997.

49.   **PACE ten years on: a review of the research**. David Brown. 1997.

Research Bulletin

The Research Bulletin is published twice each year and contains short articles on recent research.

Occasional Papers

Measurement of caseload weightings associated with the Children Act. Richard J. Gadsden and Graham J. Worsdale. 1994. (Available from the RSD Information and Publications Group).

Managing difficult prisoners: The Lincoln and Hull special units. Professor Keith Bottomley, Professor Norman Jepson, Mr Kenneth Elliott and Dr Jeremy Coid. 1994. (Available from the RSD Information and Publications Group).

The Nacro diversion initiative for mentally disturbed offenders: an account and an evaluation. Home Office, NACRO and Mental Health Foundation. 1994. (Available from the RSD Information and Publications Group.)

Probation Motor Projects in England and Wales. J P Martin and Douglas Martin. 1994.

Community-based treatment of sex offenders: an evaluation of seven treatment programmes. R Beckett, A Beech, D Fisher and A S Fordham. 1994.

Videotaping children's evidence: an evaluation. Graham Davies, Clare Wilson, Rebecca Mitchell and John Milsom. 1995.

Managing the needs of female prisoners. Allison Morris, Chris Wilkinson, Andrea Tisi, Jane Woodrow and Ann Rockley. 1995.

Local information points for volunteers. Michael Locke, Nick Richards, Lorraine Down, Jon Griffiths and Roger Worgan. 1995.

Mental disorder in remand prisoners. Anthony Maden, Caecilia J. A. Taylor, Deborah Brooke and John Gunn. 1996.

An evaluation of prison work and training. Frances Simon and Claire Corbett. 1996.

The Impact of the National Lottery on the Horse-Race Betting Levy. Simon Field. 1996.

Reviewing risk. A review of research on the assessment and management of risk and dangerousness: implications for policy and practice in the Probation Service. Hazel Kemshall. 1996. (available from IPG).

Crack cocaine and drugs - crime careers. Howard Parker and Tim Bottomley. 1996.

The social implications of casino gambling. Iain Brown and Sue Fisher (edited by Clem Henricson and Joel Miller). 1996.

Evaluation of a Home Office initiative to help offenders into employment. Ken Roberts, Alana Barton, Julian Buchanan and Barry Goldson. 1996.

Books

Analysing Offending. Data, Models and Interpretations. Roger Tarling. 1993. viii + 203pp. (0 11 341080 8).

Requests for Publications

Home Office Research Studies from 143 onwards, *Research and Planning Unit Papers, Research Findings and Research Bulletins* are available **subject to availability** on request from:

Research and Statistics Directorate
Information and Publications Group
Room 278, Home Office
50 Queen Anne's Gate
London SW1H 9AT
Telephone: 0171 273 2084
Fascimile: 0171 222 0211
Internet: http://www.open.gov.uk/home off/rsdhome.htp

Occasional Papers can be purchased from:
Home Office
Publications Unit
50 Queen Anne's Gate
London SW1H 9AT
Telephone: 0171 273 2302

Home Office Research Studies prior to 143 can be purchased from:

HMSO Publications Centre

(Mail, fax and telephone orders only)
PO Box 276, London SW8 5DT
Telephone orders: 0171-873 9090
General enquiries: 0171-873 0011
(queuing system in operation for both numbers)
Fax orders: 0171-873 8200

*And also from **HMSO Bookshops***